STUDYING AMERICAN BEAUTY

Jeremy Points

Contents

Factsheet

American Beauty	1999, USA
Running Time	122 minutes
Certificate	18
Production Companies	DreamWorks
Distributor	United International Pictures

Key credits

Director	Sam Mendes
Writer	Alan Ball
Producers	Bruce Cohen, Dan Jinks
Director of Photography	Conrad Hall
Music	Thomas Newman
Editors	Tariq Anwar, Christopher Greenbury
Costume Designer	Julie Weiss
Production Designer	Naomi Shohan

Cast

Lester Burnham	Kevin Spacey
Carolyn Burnham	Annette Bening
Jane Burnham	Thora Birch
Angela Hayes	Mena Suvari
Frank Fitts	Chris Cooper
Ricky Fitts	Wes Bentley
Barbara Fitts	Allison Janney

Synopsis

Connecticut, the present. Lester Burnham's own voice-over informs us that he will soon be dead. Neither his family nor professional life is happy, and Lester becomes obsessed with his daughter Jane's school friend, Angela. Meanwhile, Ricky – the son of the Burnhams' new neighbour, a retired marine colonel named Frank Fitts – makes videos of Jane.

Pursuing his lost youth, Lester quits work and takes a job in a fast-food restaurant. He also starts to work out and takes recreational drugs supplied by Ricky. His wife Carolyn begins an affair with her commercial rival Buddy Kane, and Jane and Ricky begin to fall in love. Lester finds out about Carolyn's affair and Buddy calls it off.

One night, Frank spies on Ricky and Lester and, mistakenly concluding that Lester is paying his son for sex, Frank assaults Ricky, who prepares to leave home with Jane. Distraught, Carolyn drives home with a loaded gun. Frank confronts Lester but ends up making an advance, which Lester sensitively refuses. Lester finally gets a chance to have sex with Angela but on finding she's a virgin, grows paternal instead. Frank enters the house and shoots Lester. At the moment of his death, Lester sees his life pass before him and realises how beautiful it has been.

Budget

$15m

Release strategy

A 'platform' release that opened in the US on just 16 screens; by week four it was showing on over 1000 screens. A similar strategy was employed in the UK where it opened on 23 screens then 'went wide' the following week.

1. Openers

Here's a still from an early scene in American Beauty – dinner accompanied by exotic music that conjures up a South Sea island paradise for Carolyn and the interior of elevators for Lester. And these are the sorts of things you might start to think about when looking at it:

textual features: micro analysis

mise-en-scène 1 – set, costume and lighting

- connotations of set – immaculate, expensive furnishing
- tasteful (?) minimalist contemporary design
- feeling and warmth suffocated by too perfect domestic décor and lighting which emphasises emotional emptiness
- costume – colder blues and greys, picks up predominant blue/grey décor
- place settings on table immaculate
- central flowers – light behind them illuminates Jane

mise-en-scène 2 – connotations of framing and composition

- symmetrical framing – husband and wife distanced by long, expensive table (literal distance equivalent to emotional distance)
- Jane positioned centrally with flowers
- intertextuality – framing alludes to Robert Redford's *Ordinary People* (1980), where a similar well-off middle-class family is exposed as repressive – Mendes uses a larger table and has more minimalist set
- almost imperceptibly slow pull-shot (zoom in) to draw in audience as family tension increases

editing

- juxtaposed with previous shot of everyday tension between husband and wife and subsequent shot of Lester trying to placate his daughter, Jane, in the kitchen

sound

- scene is bathed in music from 1950s Rodgers & Hammerstein musical, *South Pacific* (Bali Ha'i)
- emblem of conflict and image of Carolyn's management of family emotion
- dialogue

textual features: macro analysis

genre

not an icon of any particular genre

not part of obvious mainstream genre

recognise it as character-driven drama

possible links with independent films of late 90s (e.g. *The Ice Storm* (1997), *The Virgin Suicides* (1999)) that are critical of white middle-class America

narrative

- structure of scene – moving towards emotional climax
- place in narrative structure of whole film
- beginning to suggest tensions and conflict

audiences

Positioned to sympathise with Lester – preferred reading?

fans of Kevin Spacey – responding to signature dialogue?

younger audiences identifying with this minor domestic conflict?

Thora Birch familiar from *Patriot Games* (1992) or *Dungeons and Dragons* (2000)

black audiences noticing 'whiteness' of suburban middle-class *mise-en-scène* suggesting that there are different ways of interpreting the same scene?

1. Openers

Cinematography *is technically more than camerawork: it covers all aspects of camerawork, such as distance – choice of lens and depth of focus, angles and movement, as well as framing and composition, lighting and what kind and speed of film to print on.*

Micro features of a film: *mise-en-scène, cinematography, editing and sound – the main elements of film-making.*

Macro features of a film: *the way the film as a whole is organised – as a narrative and with reference to genre conventions.*

Cinematographer, *the still used (but slightly more traditional term) for Director of Photography.*

Ideology *is (roughly) the messages and values which are conveyed by a film. More on this in section 5.*

Looking closer at American Beauty

The observations on page 1 cover several different aspects of *American Beauty*, from its camerawork (or, more precisely, cinematography), editing, lighting, sets, sound and music score to its genre and narrative. Those are the familiar areas of film study, more recently called 'micro' and 'macro' features. The *micro* features cover what's sometimes called 'film language' and the macro covers the way films as a whole are organised – in terms of their narrative and genre.

The graphic also raises the question of whether all audiences interpret a scene in the same way. I don't think they necessarily do. And this brings up another important aspect of studying film: how different audiences make sense of what they see. In attempting to uncover how different audiences might make sense of *American Beauty*, I will be exploring several important film issues which are suggested by *American Beauty*: representation, realism and ideology. I'll also be going on to talk about other audience issues such as film fans and spectators as well as what it means to talk of the director, stars or the cinematographer as 'auteurs'.

Looking in a different way: breathtakingly beautiful?

Apart from looking at the film and its audiences, I want additionally to look at the film as a product of a highly sophisticated global industry (that's to say, the film's production, distribution and exhibition). The aim will be to combine considering these broader industry perspectives with asking questions about how they affect the nature of the film itself.

So in everything I do in this study guide, I'll doubtless be echoing the film's tagline: *look closer* (which, incidentally, appears pinned up in Lester's office cubicle, not unlike other messages pinned on a notice board in another Kevin Spacey film – *The Usual Suspects* (1995)).

Studying American Beauty, studying film

This guide will therefore be as much about how you study films in general as it is about *American Beauty*. So it's going to raise questions as well as attempt to answer some of them. I don't think there's one single way of studying a film but you will probably recognise that my approach is familiar from studying Film and Media at AS/A Level and is rooted in examining the film itself, the way audiences make sense of it and the way the film industry context affects not only the nature of the film but also the way audiences respond to that film.

Looking in a different way...

The film not only invites its audiences to 'look closer' but it also encourages them to look at things in a different way. Arguably the central scene in the film – Ricky's digital recording of a bag blowing in the wind in a parking lot – is a good example. Audiences might simply see a bag blowing about in the wind; the film, on the other hand, suggests that this play of bag against wind is beautiful. It needs to be seen in a different way, however, to recognise that.

I want to encourage you to be able to look at the film in a different way by suggesting both the conventional range of approaches to studying the film as well as making suggestions for putting the film in unfamiliar contexts through images and comments. In addition, I'll be promoting an active, creative approach to studying film by breaking up reading with activities at the end of each section.

2. The Look: cinematography, mise-en-scène, editing and sound

One of the most striking features of *American Beauty* is the way it *looks*. The director Sam Mendes had a clear view about how he wanted the film to look, as his detailed storyboards demonstrated; and the production designer, Naomi Shohan, was able to convert Mendes' views into film sets, significantly aided by Julie Weiss, the costume designer. However, as Mendes has himself commented, the person primarily responsible for creating the look of the film is the cinematographer, Conrad Hall, serving to reinforce how crucial the role of the cinematographer is in putting what you see on the screen.

The camerawork seems to me to be very stylised – particularly in the lighting, framing and composition Hall employs. An obvious feature of the film is the way it blends three distinct 'visual strands', as Philip Kemp puts it in a fascinating article on the film (*Sight and Sound*, January 2000). These are:

- the sharply-lit, apparently idealised scenes of suburbia, characterised by static camera positions and slow camera movement

- the more fluid, computer-generated imagery of Lester's fantasies, characterised by repeated, almost 'jump cut' shots and

- Ricky's handheld digital observations, with a grainier, supposedly more amateur look.

I'm going to call these strands the three different 'looks' of *American Beauty*. Using Sam Mendes' own words, this is how Philip Kemp distinguishes between them:

1 For the main part Mendes [creates] a 'sparse, almost surreal feeling – a bright, crisp, hard-edge, near Magritte take on American suburbia'…Mendes chose a 'very composed camera style'. 'I didn't want to use steadicam. I didn't want lots of close-ups. My camera, I realised, is a stiller, much more stealthy presence.'

2 …in the fantasy sequences the camera movements are 'more fluid and graceful'.

3 …the scenes supposedly shot by Ricky on video (most of which Mendes shot himself although some were filmed by Wes Bentley) have 'a much more kinetic, handheld, strange energy, and a different sort of poetry in the images'. (*Sight and Sound*, Jan 2000, page 24)

Each look, then, corresponds to a different aspect of the film and indeed suggests how they're linked. American suburbia is given the 'crisp' critical focus; Lester's fantasies lead to his understanding of what lies below that surface; and Ricky's images are an indication of what you might find if you look closer.

The whole effect is to show the familiar in an unfamiliar way, which forces us to look closer and in a different way – which is of course what *American Beauty* is all about. I'm going to explore these three looks as a way of uncovering the 'micro' features of the film.

Researching articles

- *Always quote and credit key sentences and phrases from sources.*

- *Explore what's suggested by some key phrases from your quotations.*

  What, for example, do you think Mendes means by:

  'a very composed camera style'

  [the camera is] 'a stiller, much more stealthy presence'?

Rene Magritte (1898–1967) *Belgian surrealist painter, whose paintings play with sexuality and representation and frequently feature blue skies and crisply painted detail.*

The Empire of Lights (1954): Magritte's version of Robin Hood Drive? Magritte includes those blue, slightly cloudy skies which run through *American Beauty* in several of his paintings

2. The Look

Look 1 – a 'near-Magritte take on American suburbia' and the opening

The opening of the main action of the film is prefaced by Ricky's digital footage of Jane. This acts as a narrative frame for the main story and in visual terms is part of that 'third look' – the handheld digital camerawork. It thus serves to emphasise the sharper focus with which we are introduced to bright, sunny and well-off suburbia.

It has a deliberately digital look – low level, supposedly natural lighting with a grainy texture to the film. After noticeably adjusting the camera frame – to stress the amateur nature of the footage – Ricky films Jane lying

Murdering Dads: would you?

down in a medium shot. The whole 30 second or so sequence is in fact one take, although as Jane moves her position towards the camera, the shot has the appearance of moving to a close-up. The medium shot allows us to overhear Jane's complaints about her father and Ricky's asking whether Jane wants him to kill her father. She moves forward to create the effect of a close-up to accentuate dramatically her response to Ricky's offer to murder her Dad: 'Would you?' she asks.

American Beauty? First view of suburbia

It is a dramatic opening to the film, the full context of which emerges later. It provides, as said, a direct contrast to the establishing shot of the main narrative – an aerial shot taken from a plane, which slowly zooms in on the Burnham household. It contrasts in light and setting (the dark light of the interior of Ricky's room contrasting with the crisp, bright light of the exterior shot); and it contrasts in sound. This opening scene is framed, in sound terms, by the loading and unloading of the digital camera's disk.

The main action introduces the slightly humorous marimba sounds, a minimalist music which echoes so much of the other kinds of minimalism you see in the film (notably the set designs and the idea of seeing a world 'in a grain of sand', to use William Blake's phrase). And it of course provides the first example of highly suggestive editing.

Other openings

These opening two scenes in fact represent a revised version of the opening which emerged in post-production and resulted from Sam Mendes' rethinking. The film was originally intended to be framed by courtroom scenes. Ricky and Jane were to be shown standing trial for the murder of Lester Burnham and these scenes were actually filmed. The film's main narrative was intended to establish their innocence.

Yet a further version started whimsically with Lester flying into his own bedroom, courtesy of the plane shot finally used for the existing second scene. According to his DVD commentary, Mendes felt that the idea of Lester flying in to tell his story from the dead turned the whole film into something more like a Coen Brothers' film. Whilst editing, Mendes realised that the film was fundamentally more dark and disturbing, despite several grotesque elements of comedy. The film could be thought of as some kind of contemporary 'tragicomedy', mixing an apparently homophobic killing with comedy and poignancy.

- *What kind of film would have been produced with the original 'frame narrative'?*
- *Would it have been more of a genre film?*
- *What is the effect for you of the current version of the opening?*

Sunset Boulevard meets Robin Hood Drive

The use of the voiceover, narrated by a dead person, is borrowed from Billy Wilder's 1951 film *Sunset Boulevard*, which is itself a neat manipulation of the conventional private eye voiceover which opened private detective thriller films from the 1940s – 'film noir' films. And there is something quite revealing about this reference: both films employ the stylised and expressive lighting associated with film noir, both are resolved by deaths and both expose the emptiness of a senseless material wealth aside the importance of human emotion. You might also say that in genre terms the original, but not quite realised, version of *American Beauty* had more of the conventions of a crime thriller about it. Whereas the death of the central, William Holden character in Sunset Boulevard is seen as a grotesque, unjustified conclusion to a 'sad loser's life', the ending of *American Beauty* is grotesque in that it reveals, right at the moment of his death, Lester's realisation that his 'stupid little life' was after all worth something.

This revealing reference to another film, which increases what a film suggests to audiences, is formally called 'intertextuality' – where one film 'text' informs the interpretation of another. Films – and indeed all forms of art and literature – employ intertextuality as a means of broadening the suggestiveness of scenes to audiences. *American Beauty* also makes a reference to Robert Redford's *Ordinary People* (1980), explicitly in the dinner table scene already referred to as well as near the end of the film where Carolyn seems to undergo some agonising recognition of what she has become in front of the closet wardrobe. In *Ordinary People*, Mary Tyler Moore plays a mother accused of emotional coldness towards her son. She similarly buckles in front of a closet wardrobe.

post-production: all the editing that takes place after filming has been completed.

Sunset Boulevard. **That's me dead: a forerunner of Lester telling his story**

Intertextuality: similar moments in *American Beauty* and *Ordinary People*

2. The Look

Establishing characters

Lester

Visually, we are introduced to Lester through a sequence of shots: the aerial shot of Lester waking up is followed by the humorous close-up of his feet being placed in some carefully positioned slippers. We then cut to the tracking shot of Lester in the shower masturbating. The dry tone of voice, with its startling sense of being deadened by the pointlessness of his daily existence and his alienation within his own family, echoes these shots. There's almost something mechanical about this morning routine, which is made funny by the marimba-style music and Lester's voiceover. The camera then slowly pans past Lester before cutting to the close-up of the 'American Beauty', the rose which is so finely cultivated by Carolyn. The camera tilts from flower to the pruning sheers Carolyn wields, before cutting to the long shot which allows us to observe (just about) the matching pruning handles and gardening clogs.

American beauties: Carolyn keeping up appearances

The visual framing is significant here. In the fascinating audio commentary to the film, Sam Mendes talks of the way Alan Ball, the screenwriter, almost unconsciously informs this early scene with images of entrapment. Lester is seen enclosed in his shower (attempting to liberate himself from everyday reality through sexuality?), enclosed in the house (looking out from behind the strongly framed window), and enclosed in the back of the car (but looking out at the open sky – once again, very Magritte-like – courtesy of a point of view shot). The sequence ends with Lester's reflection against the stream of computerised data, giving the impression of prison bars. Mendes comments that he wanted the camerawork and mise-en-scène to emphasise that feeling of being trapped.

Carolyn

The presentation of Carolyn in these early scenes is equally significant. The audience is clearly positioned to respond more positively to Lester as a person who in a humorous way recognises the emptiness of his daily life. We don't get the opportunity

to reflect on what Carolyn thinks: she is introduced by Lester, with implied point-of-view shots to accompany his voiceover. His voiceover anchors those shots and the way we consequently see Carolyn – as a woman who has channelled all spontaneity and sexuality into the superficial, manicured beauty of her garden and house. When the sound is brought up on her conversation with Jim, we hear artificially polite and inane remarks ('it's all in the eggshells and pruning'). She is portrayed as expending all her energies into nurturing this rose, which displays a superficial beauty – an 'American Beauty'. This is in keeping with the world of image identified with Carolyn and revealed as superficial as the film progresses.

Already, a narrative point has been established: both Carolyn and Lester have been effectively pressurised into conformity. They are both repressed in different ways: Lester by his work and the material drive he associates with Carolyn and family demands; Carolyn through having sublimated all her energies into creating an immaculately furnished house and a perfectly tended garden with its conspicuously beautiful roses.

This exterior scene of a materially comfortable middle-class makes an interesting comparison with David Lynch's *Blue Velvet* (1986). They both use:

- overexposed light
- immaculate lawns
- intensely coloured flowers set against white picket fences.

In *Blue Velvet*, this becomes the occasion for a surreal exploration of the unconscious desires which are actively repressed by bland middle-class conformity. In *American Beauty* the consequences of those repressions are acted out for us. Lester and Carolyn both attempt to liberate themselves from repression whilst Fitts becomes its victim. He kills as a result of his repressed sexuality.

Jane

Lester then introduces Jane. Immediately there's a contrast in mise-en-scène – warmer lighting and warmer oranges and reds of both room and computer screen. She is shown downloading advice on breast enlargement whilst revealing the first of several shots of characters in front of mirrors. The sequence again anticipates the issues raised by the film: Jane is effectively being pressurised into conforming to the stereotype of a superficial 'American Beauty' (embodied by her friend Angela) and judges herself in that way in the mirror. Later mirror shots – a reflection, as it were, of Ricky's interest in her – reveal that Jane learns to rebel against that pressure to conform to the American Beauty ideal and be more satisfied with her own physical appearance. Indeed, when she reveals her breasts to Ricky – or is it just to his observational camera? – it serves as an indication not only of trust but of a confident recognition that there is nothing wrong with her own body.

Carolyn's scowl

The final sequence of this scene brings together the whole family – and it is one which visually reinforces how Lester and Carolyn view each other. The reverse shots, first of all from Carolyn to Jane, emphasise Carolyn's control: 'Are you trying to look ugly? Congratulations, darling – you've succeeded admirably.' That is visually underlined with the hint a jump cut in the cutaway (Jane arrives in medium close-up in exaggerated time). The equivalent shot with Lester – who predictably drops the contents of his case – provides Carolyn with the opportunity to scowl at him with effortless superiority. The low angle point-of-view shot looking up at Carolyn's scowling face emphasises Lester's role as 'clown' of the family. These roles and camera shots are reversed later at Mr Smiley's when Lester is able to look down on Carolyn, almost disinterestedly, when pointing out that 'she can *never* tell him what to do again'.

Look 1 – so far...

This opening uses the full range of micro features – cinematography, mise-en-scène, editing and sound – to create the 'near Magritte take on American suburbia'. The cinematography is indeed highly composed, as lighting and framing are both stylised to produce this 'stiller, stealthier' presence. The stealth seems to be in the eye of the understated, critical observer. The camera doesn't just show – it exposes characters and their beautiful but superficial worlds. We are thus positioned to be critical of the world portrayed.

A closer look at Look 1 – dinner in the South Pacific

A similar kind of cinematography, supported by sound, editing and mise-en-scène, is used as a 'stealthy presence' to expose characters in the early family dinner scene mentioned in the introductory section. Have a look back at the graphic (pg. 1).

This time, let's start by focusing on sound: luscious, exotic music emerges, having overlapped with the previous scene of marital bickering between Lester and Carolyn. (It is a common editing technique for sound to anticipate image and 'bridge' the cut from one scene to another – hence a 'sound bridge'.) It's from the Rodgers and Hammerstein musical, *South Pacific*, and provides a touch of the South Pacific in a suburban living room, thereby gently mocking its inhabitants. It is thus a use of music, which does more than simply accompany. It is identified as Carolyn's music – and we smile at her expense. It's her pretension to create the perfect relaxing, paradisal atmosphere for the family evening dinner, a set piece in itself. Even the choice of this (light) classical music – which starkly contrasts with the Bobby Darin she triumphantly sings later ('Don't Rain on my Parade') – seems to have a sense of aspiration about it. It's as though she has chosen music which is not quite classical but meant nevertheless to confer 'class' on the scene.

A touch of the *South Pacific* for dinner?

This use of sound – diegetic, as the sound is a part of the film's narrative – is a reminder of the way music, like camerawork, editing and mise-en-scène, can also reveal elements about a character or a scene as well as punctuate a narrative. And music is a very important aspect of this film. Thomas Newman's score is to me perfectly judged and has become something of an icon, having been sampled in various dance mixes and advertisements. He creates sound worlds which act like 'leitmotifs'. There are, for example, the creative percussion and marimba sounds

2. The Look

Diegesis: *the word for narrative. Diegetic sound is thus sound and music which appears in the film's narrative, like Steeler's Wheel 'Stuck in the Middle with You' in* Reservoir Dogs *(1992). Non-diegetic sound is outside the narrative.*

Leitmotif: *a musical term from the world of opera, where a theme symbolises a character or idea (used most notably by Richard Wagner, 1813–1883, in his operas) and is heard each time that character appears.*

Thomas Newman: *cousin of pop musician Randy Newman, who recently won an Oscar for 'If I Didn't Have You' from* Monster's Inc *(2002) - also produced the music for Alan Ball's TV series* Six Feet Under, *Sam Mendes' next film,* Road to Perdition *(2002) and* Finding Nemo *(2003).*

Cold comfort: parents and daughter

associated with Lester's humorous and unconventional take on suburban conformity, the detuned mandolin and percussion used for Lester's fantasy sequences and the haunting piano tones associated with the revelation of a beauty which is not superficial, often accompanying Ricky and Jane.

The music sets the scene. But before you see the family themselves, we are shown some close-ups of family photographs – all of them featuring Jane and finishing with a formally-posed 'family' photograph. The family photo in particular seems to reflect how Carolyn and Lester, like all parents, want to think of themselves – as a loving family. But of course the connotations of the image are exactly the opposite. The very formality of the pose suggests coldness rather than warmth. It's very obviously an idealised image. And that's exactly what we see in the family at the dinner table.

Like the photograph, the composition is perfectly posed and symmetrical, almost as if it *were* a photograph. The shot starts as a long shot of the family, with the immaculate dining table, 'dressed' with the central vase of 'red' roses. Lester and Carolyn sit – at some distance, almost at the edge of the frame – with Jane behind the central vase of flowers, with her head just above them. Surrounding that is a dining room that is 'tastefully' furnished in a minimalist way, with a colour scheme of blues and greys, a colour 'palette' echoed in the dress of Carolyn and Lester; Carolyn in smart casual clothes and Lester in a grey singlet, which makes him look weak and a little ridiculous. There is no colour in anybody's cheeks and the whole scene is lit to accentuate this effect (Conrad Hall actually placed a small light behind the vase of flowers to pick up Jane and cast shadows).

I've mentioned these references to sound, set and lighting to establish the scene. (Sets, lighting and costume are, of course, described formally as 'mise-en-scène', which is the French for 'put on stage' [scène means 'stage', not 'scene', in French], and includes everything which is placed on the set in preparation for filming.) Turning to the camerawork reveals an extraordinary shot. At first you don't appreciate it but the initial long shot, framed by the entrance to the room itself, gradually turns into a very slow zoom to a medium close-up of the family. The whole shot takes just over a minute and represents the gradual revelation of the family tensions as well as being a virtually iconic echo of the film's exhortation to 'look closer'. As we gradually become more familiar with this family, we see they're not the ideal family of the photographs which precede the scene. They represent the 'average dysfunctional' family of today's America (and elsewhere?), which, as audiences, we seem to respond to as more plausible for today. It's certainly familiar from several films past and present – *Ordinary People* (which influenced the whole film and this scene in particular), *The Virgin Suicides*, *The Ice Storm*, *Happiness* (1998), to say nothing of *The Simpsons*.

The sequence seems to sum up the breathtaking look of the film – stylised camerawork, highly expressive lighting, minimalist and thus highly suggestive set design. Sam Mendes has talked about his constant request to 'empty the frame', commenting that he was 'obsessed with just clearing things out' and thought his 'production designer would kill [him]' (quoting again from Philip Kemp's article in *Sight and Sound*, Jan 2000).

NOTES:

Look 2 (*fantasy*) – 'more fluid and graceful camera' movements

When it comes to exploring the way Lester's fantasies are created, there are perhaps four main elements:

- the slow motion, as if time is suspended;

- the kind of repeated jump cut (a technique more frequently seen in action films);

- the sparse lighting;

- and the sounds of the detuned mandolin and percussion.

This can be seen in the basketball sequence, where Lester first sees Angela. The choreography sets up how Lester's attention is going to be drawn to Angela: the cheerleaders peel off to reveal Angela to Lester's gaze. Slow zooms are used on both Angela and Lester, to reveal Lester staring in a frankly lustful, even voyeuristic way (an interesting comparison with Ricky's camerawork). This leads up to the repeated jump cut effect as Angela first of all smoothes down her body with open palms in a blatantly sexual way and then grasps her zipped jacket as if to reveal her breasts. This shot, of clenched hands pulling at her zipped top, is repeated four times before the computer-generated rose petals are actually released in exaggeratedly slow motion. The micro features here emphasise that we have entered Lester's psychological world of desire and fantasy – but there is curiously something calm and serene about it. The fantasy seems to suggest contemplation – like the calm that will eventually come to him at the moment of his death and his realisation of everything he has in his 'stupid little life'.

Releasing (Lester's) desires

The same features are used in the later sequence in the kitchen. The shots on this occasion convey the sensual effect on Lester's

fantasies of Angela brushing her hand against him. Again the moment of the touch is conveyed by the same kind of repeated jump cut which features in all the fantasy sequences and which culminates in the appearance of a rotational shot – actually filmed by keeping the camera fixed and rotating Angela and Lester on a moving platform.

There is thus a visual and stylistic unity between all the fantasy shots. But in addition to that, there's a link between Lester's own fantasy images and the near-Magritte world of his daily existence. For *the* icon of Lester's fantasies is the shot of Angela naked in the bed of rose petals. This is, as Mendes has himself said, very like the world of a Magritte painting. It's as though Lester's and Carolyn's life is being made surreal to invite us – like a Magritte painting – to see it with fresh eyes. We are being led to look closer and see past the surface of their lives just as they are.

Look 3 (Ricky's 'voyeuristic' filming) – the more kinetic, handheld look with its strange energy

Let's consider what's suggested by the way Mendes describes the micro features of Ricky's obsessive filming:

> '[Ricky's filmed scenes have a] much more kinetic, handheld, strange energy and a different sort of poetry in the images.'   (Mendes in Strick, 2000)

- ***more kinetic*** – 'kinetic' means movement, i.e., the camerawork appears to involve more movement than the composed, static shots of the main action of the film.

- ***handheld*** – some slight hand adjustments are visible but Ricky's camerawork is not handheld in the way that, say, Dogme films are. Think of the difference between the suggestively disruptive and violent handheld camerawork of *Breaking the Waves*

icon: *technically an image which resembles what it symbolises. It is used more loosely in media and film as an image which becomes totally identified with the events or issues it represents. For example, the camerawork in the dinner scene stands for the tagline to 'look closer'.*

McDonalds has become an icon of consumerisation and globalisation.

The Spartanettes' dance routine was choreographed by 80s popstar Paula Abdul

2. The Look

Ricky's filming does have the amateur handheld look of that iconic moment of voyeuristic filming – the opening of Michael Powell's Peeping Tom *(1960). Powell was aiming to link the voyeurism of cinema spectators with the voyeurism of a psychopath.*

More about voyeurism and film in section 6, Spectators.

Looking closer: Ricky's voyeuristic camera or just reaching out?

Jane challenging 'asshole'

Jane's smile: acceptance of Ricky's attentions

(1996), *Festen* (1998) or *The Idiots* (1998) and the gentler handheld digital camerawork Ricky uses in this film. This kind of handheld camerawork was incidentally popularised on television through Steve Bochco's *NYPD Blue*, where it was intended to suggest a more intense form of realism.

• The one scene where there is very obvious 'kinetic, handheld' camerawork is when Ricky's father, Colonel Fitts, strikes Ricky in rage. The camera movement suggests the emotional frenzy and violence of the action.

• *strange energy/a different sort of poetry* – this is most obviously seen in what Ricky films; the dead bird, the bag dancing in the wind. I think the 'strange energy and … poetry', however, comes from the way Ricky constantly zooms in for close-ups. The poetry comes as a result of *looking closer*. He constantly zooms in past the superficially beautiful – when he, for example, zooms in through the window past the exhibitionist Angela to pick up an extreme close-up of Jane's gently smiling face in the bedroom table mirror. But it also happens when Jane bares her breasts for Ricky and his camera. Ricky zooms in for a close-up of her face, ignoring her exposed breasts. He also constantly zooms in to fix his – and our – attention on what he finds beautiful or interesting.

Of all the above features, it's the tendency to zoom in quickly which I think is most significant. Ricky's camerawork is full of 'looking closer' and capturing the unconventionally beautiful. There are several instances of this. Look at the first occasion when Ricky openly films Jane, after the basketball game. Jane gets out of

the car and we initially see Ricky's camera acting like a suspicious, voyeuristic presence. The first shot is a 45 degree long shot with a slight adjustment of the zoom – actually slightly pulling out – before quite rapidly zooming in as he slowly pans to follow (pursue?) Jane up the path.

It's *his* point of view and it's of course set up to make us think that he's being the 'perv' Angela thinks he is. It has all the features of the voyeuristic. To emphasise that, you return to the 'natural' filming of Jane's point of view as she looks towards the totally dark porch from where Ricky is filming. There's a pause before Ricky pulls the light cord to reveal himself and Jane challenges him by shouting across 'asshole'. After that reverse shot, we return to Jane on film. Once again, she's the apparent object of Ricky's voyeuristic gaze. The later shots of Jane inside the house – with some dolly shots which almost echo the slow pans of Ricky's filming - end up with a close-up on Jane against the curtain. The light is increased slightly to reveal the lower part of Jane's face, just enough to reveal her gentle smile. She's not threatened by Ricky's attention but is flattered by it. The shot reveals that she accepts his filming is not as 'pervy' as it appears and represents a desire to reach out and get closer to her. So his camerawork is not the kind of voyeuristic filming which gives power to men and subjugates women. Indeed, it gives her the strength to have confidence in her own image. She actually gains power from his attention. If you look at the digital camerawork elsewhere, it's relatively still but full of the desire to 'look closer'.

So these three 'looks' – three visual strands – all therefore underline the central issues the film explores. They also hint at a way of exploring realism – which I'll be considering in the section on representation.

NOTES:

2. The Look – Worksheet 1

Task

- Read the simplified version of the opening of *American Beauty* below.

- Describe how you would introduce the two main characters, Lester and Carolyn, who live in a wealthy, leafy suburb of an American city in TEN shots.

- You are *not* allowed to use any shots used by Sam Mendes and Conrad Hall.

- If stuck look at the prompts below to help get you started:

The opening

Lester (voiceover)

Hello. I'm Lester Burnham. In a year I'm going to be dead. Except I don't know that yet, of course. But it probably doesn't matter as in a way, I'm dead already. This is me looking out of the window at my wife. She's looking after her roses. See the way the handles of the gardening shears match her boots. That's not an accident.

Prompts: the main scenes

1: Establishing shot of house where Lester and Carolyn live – what kind of establishing shot?

2: Lester – in bedroom – camera distance, angle, position?

3: Lester looks out of window to Carolyn tending to her roses.

Camerawork and sound

Try to incorporate all the main variables of filming: distance, angle/position & movement. You could also decide to have some low level music below the voiceover.

Compare your version with the actual opening of the film, from Ricky filming Jane to the moment when Lester is shown at his work cubicle. What conclusions can you draw about the differences between Mendes' and your own approaches?

If you have a DVD with Sam Mendes' and Alan Ball's sound commentary, find out what Sam Mendes says about this opening.

2. The Look – Worksheet 2

Exploring the micro features of *American Beauty*

A typical task (which lies at the root of all film analyses)

Focus on how *one or more* of mise-en-scène, cinematography, editing and sound create meaning and generate response in a film sequence of no more than 7 minutes. (If the sequence is a complex one, it may be much shorter than 7 minutes.)

Approaching the task

Getting the focus right

- Choose a sequence which has made a particular impact on you or one which is very significant – often the beginning, ending or a climactic moment.

- Identify what precisely made the most impact on you and say why.

- Use your conclusions to select the feature(s) you will concentrate on (for example, mise-en-scène or cinematography).

Starting to analyse

- Produce a precise shot by shot analysis of your sequence, using the plan below (effectively a storyboard without pictures).

- Choose approximately THREE to FIVE key sequences of shots and explore what is suggested by your chosen area (what are the connotations of sets, camera shots, lighting etc.).

- Always ask what is *suggested to you and to audiences in general* by the features you're analysing.

- It may be possible to print some still images of shots from the scene(s) you are analysing. This is particularly useful for identifying all the elements of mise-en-scène (e.g., sets & locations, lighting, costume, facial expression and/or make-up).

- Always watch again sequences you are analysing to check your conclusions.

Organising your final analysis

- *Start with a brief introductory overview of the two most important ideas you have discovered. For example: 'The formal framing and composed camera style emphasises the obsession with image and appearance...'*

- *Write a paragraph on each major sequence of shots you are exploring.*

- *Aim to explore and develop one or two ideas rather than simply describe what happens.*

- *Check that you are concentrating on what the micro-feature you are exploring suggests, why it is used and why it has created impact.*

Shot Number	Time Line (seconds)	Brief Description of *mise-en-scène* (include lighting)	Description of Camera Shots (include framing & composition when analysing in more detail)	Description of Sound

2. The Look – Worksheet 3

Going further with your analysis

More research

- Your own ideas might be extended by researching what others have said about cinematography, mise-en-scène, editing or sound generally.

- Similarly you might find other people's writing on individual films helps you develop your own ideas.

- When researching other people's writing, aim to choose THREE key sentences or phrases which you might quote in your own writing.

- If you like spider diagrams, write the sentence in the middle of a page and produce a spider diagram of all the ideas suggested by the key phrase or sentence. This will help you build up ideas.

- Always quote and credit your sources like this:

  Philip Kemp, 'The Iceman Cometh', *Sight and Sound*, January 2000

  www.americanbeauty.com

  Patrick Phillips, *Understanding Film* (BFI, 2000)

- Never simply copy from sources without crediting where the information comes from.

- Always view the film sequence you are analysing after you have completed research so that you can clearly relate ideas you have uncovered to the film extract itself.

More on interpretations: audience positioning

It may be possible to reflect the fact that not all audiences will respond to the same extract in the same way. Perhaps we should talk more of how cinematography, mise-en-scène, editing and sound create meanings not just *meaning*. Your own analysis may offer different interpretations. (See section 6 on Spectators for more on this.)

When building into your analyses different interpretations of the same scene, I suggest the following:

- choose a particular moment/sequence of shots in the extract to anchor your possible different interpretations;

- think in terms of *preferred* interpretations – how the majority of audiences are positioned to respond to a particular scene – *oppositional or negotiated* interpretations;

- try to account for how a group of people may develop an oppositional or negotiated interpretation.

Different interpretations of Bud and Carolyn's dinner rendezvous

- *Preferred interpretation*: Audiences are invited to laugh at Carolyn as we see the growing intimacy developing between Carolyn and Bud. Although the scene represents the chance for Carolyn to assert her independence and liberate herself from the mundane relationship she has with Lester, the scene suggests something ridiculous, which is confirmed in the later sex scene and gun shooting scene, which suggest parody. This is partly because the audience (male-oriented?) has already been positioned to laugh at Carolyn and underwrite Lester's aspirations to sleep with Angela.

- *Oppositional interpretation*: Some audiences – possibly female – may see that Carolyn has indeed become a victim of materialism and is desperately trying to shock herself into a new kind of life. This interpretation is likely to be much more sympathetic to Carolyn and challenge the dominant view of the film.

Testing the oppositional interpretation

- what would the film look like rescripted from Carolyn's point of view, with Carolyn taking on Lester's role (with all the best lines/attracted to Ricky?) and Lester the materialism-driven sales executive more concerned with house, garden and home cinema system?

- does this have implications for the way women and men are represented in the film?

See section 4 on Representations for more on this.

3. Narrative and genre

narrative: not only a story but also the act of telling a story...

film narrative: telling a story in pictures

The basics about narratives

The word 'narrative' means not only a story but also the act of telling a story. That is a good way of starting to think about film narratives: for a film narrative in a very basic sense is telling a story in pictures. **It also reminds you that film narratives are ways of** organising **images and scenes into a film. In a very literal sense, a film's narrative is finally established in the editing room – as part of post-production. As I've already mentioned, this happened in a dramatic way with *American Beauty* – the narrative changed from a teenagers-on-trial drama to a story based on the apparent mid-life crisis of a murdered man. In other words, film narratives are constructed in order to tell a story. And the power of stories, in whatever form, is that they create responses and meanings – they elicit responses from us, suggest ideas and raise issues.**

You might distinguish between two areas to explore when analysing narratives:

- how the narrative is constructed to generate a response in audiences – which you can see by looking at individual scenes;

- how the narrative of a complete film is structured – which has become the subject of several theories (by writers like Todorov and Lévi-Strauss, for example).

I think both of those points remind you that narratives do more than simply tell stories. They tend not only to show but to imply a point of view about what's being shown. To put it formally, in terms which will hopefully become familiar later, narratives are ideological representations which reinforce points of view about people, groups of people and thus the contemporary world we all live in. You could go further and claim that most narratives reinforce in quite basic ways a belief in causality – that all behaviour can be understood in terms of cause and effect.

How the narrative is constructed

Let's start to work out how *American Beauty*'s narrative is constructed visually. First of all, think about the opening.

> *Openings establish characters and locations – which are normally designed to tell audiences more about the characters in the narrative.*
>
> - What do you learn about Carolyn and how is that information conveyed visually?
>
> - Replay the sequence with the sound down to concentrate just on the visual information.
>
> - Look back at section 2 to compare what we said about Carolyn there. Note: it is the micro-features which initially establish character.

What that tells you is that narratives are constructed through images, which are placed next to one another in a connected sequence. We normally talk of **juxtaposing** images, where juxtaposition literally means placing images 'side by side'. Let's focus on Carolyn's determined attempts to sell the house ('I am going to sell this house today') to see this narrative construction at work. (DVD timing – scene 3, 9:52 - 13:15 mins.)

NOTES:

This is in essence a simple story. Estate agent with her own business tries and fails to sell a house. But notice immediately that the images tell more than the mere story: they are constantly building up information about Carolyn.

The first sequence in this scene tells a mini-story in itself. And it's effectively created by a simple repetition of shots – cutting between two main shots:

- The estate agent sign: it tells of a woman with her own business and suggests a positive mental outlook for the day ahead as she takes out cleaning equipment from her car in the early morning sun.

- Cut to Carolyn's first glimpse of what we later realise is Carolyn's main competitor, Buddy Kane. Cutting between the two signs shows how they contrast with one another.

- Cut back to Carolyn for reaction shot.

- Cut again to (slightly longer) shot of the Buddy Kane sign.

- Cut back to slightly longer reaction shot of Carolyn with sigh.

Images, their denotations and connotations – a story of editing

Literally, the sequence shows a female estate agent seeing another's signs; that's the denotation of the images.

But what precisely is the story being told? Audiences work that out from the connotations of the images and the way they've been edited. Carolyn sees the confident photographic image of Buddy Kane, realises his commercial superiority and admires both his success and possibly the man himself. After her sigh, she resigns herself, however, to her task with determination.

That story is established through:

- the power and connotations of visual images (the camera shots);

- the duration of each shot;

- the distance, angle and movement of the camera shots;

- the composition and framing of shots and;

- their juxtaposition (how they're edited together).

Connections

Another simple point about this moment is that you are being reminded of the earlier scene where Carolyn and Lester comment on how the house next door was sold by her arch-competitor (the same, 'great' Buddy Kane). Equally, the scene anticipates the moment where we as audiences meet Buddy Kane at the Estate Agents' party, which is itself an anticipation of the relationship which Carolyn and Buddy will have.

These observations establish another important point about narratives: that they are constantly setting up expectations and possible connections with other points in the film. As with genres, narratives create involvement through a process of establishing expectations and either fulfilling or challenging them.

The main way a film narrative is constructed, therefore, is through editing together a sequence of camera shots. And the nature of those shots and what they suggest is crucial to that narrative.

Positioning: the images tell the story

Narratives involve us; but they also position us. What view of Carolyn do we get from this sequence? That she's determined, strains for success and yet is vulnerable? That's what the narrative

A mini adventure? This mini-narrative tells a story in six shots.

3. Narrative and genre

Bordwell & Thompson, in Film Art: an Introduction, describe this kind of anticipation as parallelism – where a section of the narrative draws parallels with other parts of the film.

It's all a little like soap operas and other TV dramas. As audiences we see that the different storylines of soap operas echo one another and become a means of exploring an issue.

seems to be telling us at this moment but it also makes us laugh – and laugh at Carolyn. Why does that happen?

It's again partly to do with the way the narrative is structured. There is first of all the role of the script (the repetitions of 'I will sell this house today'). Then there's the frantic cleaning of the house, the humour of which is emphasised by camera angles and position. For example,

'I will sell this house today.' Frantic cleaning (in American Beauty red satin slip)

there's the medium close-up of Carolyn methodically and determinedly cleaning the window. There's a further medium shot of her hand cleaning the kitchen counter, followed by Carolyn emerging from behind it. And then there is the rhythmic pace of the editing as we see a parade of viewers passing by in sheer bewilderment as they try to match Carolyn's sales pitch with what they see. The selection of shots punctures the sales pitch, as for example the feature chimney piece which 'a little cream' would bring out. And we are positioned to laugh at Carolyn through the shots of her unzipping her dress to reveal her satin red slip – an American Beauty red - and vacuuming in jerky rhythms against the plain orange background. Mise-en-scène creates the humour here.

So the micro elements all contribute to encouraging the audience to find Carolyn funny, possibly even pathetic. The

Preparing a face to meet the faces you meet: the welcoming *image*

narrative is constructed to convey a point of view about Carolyn and therefore to position the audience. The conclusion of the sequence where she is preparing to receive the viewers emphasises that positioning but also shows how narratives reach out to make connections with other elements of the narrative and raises further ideas in audiences' minds.

Carolyn applies lipstick (a close-up mirror shot, much used in the film – to emphasise image, surface and the need to impress) and ostentatiously opens the double doors (which take up the complete frame) to welcome the first viewers.

This sequence emphasises image or, more precisely, the *superficiality of images*. Carolyn creates a superficial image of an attractive house at the same time as creating a superficial image of herself through make-up and subsequent behaviour. These two versions of superficial images link with the main idea the narrative constructs: that surface images mask true value and that American society is fuelled by image and materialism rather than a sense of genuine human value.

The narrative is thus building up significance gradually – it accumulates its significance by allowing audiences to establish links between comparable elements in the film.

NOTES:

Fulfilling and contradicting expectations

You might say that this view of Carolyn has already been anticipated by the film's opening and Lester's introduction of Carolyn. So the narrative is fulfilling expectations which have already been planted in audiences' minds. However, narratives also surprise by contradicting those expectations.

The scene closes with Carolyn suddenly breaking down and crying – lighting and close-up camerawork accentuate the effect. She slaps herself on the face with a determination to be stoic, which makes the scene painfully funny. And it is given extraordinary emphasis – the shot is held for 44 seconds, with no cuts or change of lighting.

That emphasis is once again created through editing – this time it is the very length of shot which is designed to get audience reaction. In the context of this film (and contemporary films in general) the concentration on one shot for this length of time is very distinctive. The audience is being forced to reflect on the significance of Carolyn's emotions.

What do they suggest? Is there a hint that the obsessive drive to sell and her even more obsessive cleaning actions are a kind of sublimated sexuality? Just as Angela is able to observe from Lester's behaviour that Lester and Carolyn have not had sex for some time, so audiences will doubtless see that Carolyn is channelling her (sexual) energies into her business and her need for status, materialism and image rather than to Lester and her relationship with him. Having established Lester's numbness, here is a sense of Carolyn's life being equally unfulfilled, needing some kind of liberating relationship and sex – which she does, of course, later have with the real estate competitor she looks up to and whose image she had been pondering earlier in this scene.

This image of emotional breakdown anticipates the later scene where Carolyn breaks down in front of her closet wardrobe and the mantra-like determination to 'sell [the] house today' is later echoed by the assertion-tape phrases she shouts in the car towards the end of the film – that she won't be a victim.

This is another example of the way the narrative suggests ideas through a system of visual referencing to other comparable narrative moments.

Editing: 44 seconds to think about Carolyn's emotions

Summary

So far, I've claimed that narratives:

- are constructed through the juxtaposition of connected visual images.

- suggest ideas and raise issues through the connotations of individual shots as well as through visual referencing to other elements of the narrative.

- are designed to involve audiences.

- play on assumptions audiences make and raise expectations.

- position audiences and thus suggest points of view about what is seen on screen.

Narrative design

I've already suggested that the way individual scenes are constructed gives an introduction to considering narratives as a whole. In other words, what you see within the 'narrative' of a short scene, you can also observe occurring in the film as a whole. The fact that narratives generate a response through the way different *elements* of narrative interrelate, and how audiences are positioned, emphasises the fact that audiences take in more than a simple story. They are assimilating attitudes, values and beliefs – ideologies – all at the same time.

Conventional ways of considering narrative design usually refer to a range of theories, most of which were developed in relation to literary, rather than film, narratives. However they do indicate some important areas to consider. So let's look at how the narrative of a complete film is structured before demonstrating how the narrative of *American Beauty* itself is constructed.

3. Narrative and genre

Back to basics: on narratives

As with all kinds of stories – whether they're fairy tales, stories we tell one another, news stories or soap operas – we bring a number of assumptions to them in order to make sense of them. Here are some of the obvious ones:

- stories have a beginning, middle and end;

- many stories have some kind of 'happy ending';

- most of us actually prefer stories with happy endings;

- we expect them to make sense and follow a kind of logic.

In other words, one immediate point you can make about narratives is that they are a way of shaping events into some kind of form, which is meant to 'interest', even 'entertain', an audience. You could go one stage further and say that stories in general are ways in which we make sense of experience and the world we live in – they provide us with ways of showing why people do things.

If you translate some of those assumptions into films, you might come up with these points:

- most films do have a beginning, middle and end and most – particularly mainstream films – do have a 'happy ending';

- most films tell their stories in a linear way and do follow a kind of logic – one piece of action leads to another, following a pattern of cause and effect;

- we don't have a lot of difficulty in understanding stories which are not strictly linear – notably those told in flashback;

- more recently, we have even become more used to non-linear narratives in films which tell stories from different points of view, but that is felt to be a little more experimental (e.g. *Pulp Fiction* (1994));

- stories which involve dream structures are often perceived as being much more confusing and are generally less common (*Blue Velvet*, *Lost Highway* (1997), *Mulholland Drive* (2001), *Fight Club* (1999), *The Usual Suspects*);

- we often take sides in stories and tend to identify with some characters more than others – notably the good and bad characters of most mainstream films;

- stories embody ways of understanding why events occur and why people act in the way they do – because they allow us to observe people.

You are probably familiar with most of these points. They are generally explored through a range of theories. I'll quickly convert those points to the theories with which they are generally associated.

Beginnings, middles and endings: Aristotle and Todorov

Aristotle drew attention to the fact that narratives had a definite structure, which made them different from everyday life, which was simply that of having a definite shape – a beginning, middle and an end. More recently, the Bulgarian Tzvetan Todorov studied a range of narratives and claimed that narratives involved slightly more than beginnings, middles and endings – they tended to conform to a common pattern, which he described in terms of restoring an

3. Narrative and genre

3. Narrative and genre

equilibrium – a sense of balance – which had been disrupted in some way:

- Establishing an equilibrium – an image of society or life as balanced and thus normal (beginning);

- Disruption of that equilibrium through some kind of disturbing event (marking the completion of the opening and the start of the middle);

- Attempt to restore that equilibrium (the attempt to restore – the middle; restored equilibrium – the ending).

Another simple way of putting this is that narratives often involve disturbing events which are eventually resolved in a 'happy ending'. This kind of pattern is seen in conventional crime or horror films: life is normal, someone is killed and the police strive to catch the perpetrator and restore order. Or: a threatening alien terrorises a community until it is finally destroyed and normal life can be resumed.

That the majority of mainstream film narratives follow this pattern probably means we develop basic beliefs about people and the societies we live in through narratives. Crudely put, mainstream narratives reinforce the idea that 'bad' people who disrupt everyday life will receive justice and that normality will always be restored. Narratives tend to reinforce the idea that normality is indeed the 'norm' and that anything which disrupts it can eventually be defeated.

Lévi-Strauss

Claude Lévi-Strauss, an anthropologist who looked at common narrative structures embedded in myths and traditional stories from a range of societies, felt that narratives were ways of resolving problems imaginatively which couldn't be resolved in society. They deceive us, in other words. He suggested that all stories place opposites in conflict – 'binary opposites' or pairs of opposites – and that the story is resolved with one element triumphing over the other. In horror films, for example, lots of elements stand for good and lots stand for evil – good is shown triumphing over evil by the end of the film.

Again, the underlying point about Lévi-Strauss' narrative theories has to do with what people believe in society. Narratives in fictional films

end by resolving conflicts which often can't be resolved in real life. They have the effect of insulating audiences from reality. Think of crime films: most tend to end with the murderer being killed or caught (*Se7en* (1995) is an exception in challenging this idea): in 'real' life, however, only a small percentage of murderers are actually caught and brought to justice. And in the majority of cases, it is chance, rather than the logical powers of investigators, which leads to arrest (*Se7en* also incorporates this far from reassuring idea).

Roland Barthes

Barthes emphasised more than other theorists how narratives work like 'codes'. He implied that narratives communicated with audiences because they had assimilated ways of understanding film codes – enigma, action and symbolic codes. The underlying thrust of what he said was that audiences bring a considerable range of assumptions to films which allow them to make sense of film narratives.

Vladimir Propp and Victor Shklovsky

I'll briefly mention two other theorists: Vladimir Propp claimed that narratives tended to deal with a basic set of characters who all had specific functions. And Victor Shklovsky made a distinction between story – the complete version of the story, with all the backgrounds to characters and events which aren't shown in the film itself – and the plot, the narrative which is actually shown in the film. The fundamental point about Shklovsky's distinction is that it stresses the fact that the 'narrative' of a film – what Shklovsky called 'plot' - is a selection of the most significant elements of the complete story which are needed to convey it. Audiences infer the rest – or recognise that what is missed out isn't relevant. It also, however, suggests that some parts of the story are given more prominence than others and again draws attention to the fact that a film narrative is something artificial and shaped for a particular reason.

Other structures

If you talk to screenwriters themselves – and Sam Mendes refers to this in his audio commentary on the *American Beauty* DVD – they talk in terms of a *three act structure*, which was actually borrowed from the characteristic structure of 19th century melodramas which provided the Hollywood film industry with many of its narratives in

American Beauty | **NARRATIVE AND GENRE**   19

3. Narrative and genre

the early years of cinema. (Much 20th century drama also uses this structure.) This structure places the emphasis on character development:

- 'Act 1' establishes character and action and frequently ends with an event which suggests change;
- 'Act 2' shows how the characters develop and change;
- 'Act 3' shows how events lead to some kind of climax.

You can see that quite visibly in *American Beauty*, where a shot of Robin Hood drive with Lester's voiceover punctuates each act. The three acts are framed by some action at the very beginning and at the end, turning the central narrative into a flashback. This is also quite a common structuring device and was notably used in *Sunset Boulevard*, which, as I've already mentioned, *American Beauty* refers to in several ways.

- 'Act 1' ends with Lester's bedroom confrontation with Carolyn, following his masturbatory bathroom fantasy (at approx. 44 mins).
- 'Act 2' ends with the scene where Jane takes Ricky's camera and films him (at approx. 1hr 15 mins). This scene also contextualises the film's opening, when we see Jane through Ricky's camera.
- 'Act 3' ends, of course, with the film's climax – Lester's murder and post-mortem voice-over (approx. 1hr 45 mins).

Putting the theories and the structures to work

Each of these theories about narrative structure seems to emphasise different aspects of the narrative. However, they all point to a slightly unconventional narrative, which leaves crucial issues unresolved at the end of the film. Have a look at the notes I've made on each:

Screenwriters' three act structure: emphasising character change but without complete resolution?

- *American Beauty* does follow the three act structure, which makes the film accessible and easy to follow. However, despite the conventional narrative structure, this is quite an unconventional narrative, which raises as many questions as it resolves.

- All the major characters undergo some kind of transformation but in ways which raise questions: Lester dies at the moment of his recognition of the wonder of his family; Carolyn comes to a realisation of her obsessive emphasis on material values and her love of Lester just as he dies; Ricky and Jane achieve freedom with an uncertain future; Angela keeps her delusory sense of herself intact, but in a way which audiences sympathise with; Barbara Fitts is left to survive in her continuing disorientation; and the narrative leaves unanswered why Fitts killed Lester, which suggests his homophobia, rooted in repression, is unresolved.

Todorov: equilibrium or just an apparent equilibrium restored?

- The film does start with some precarious sense of **equilibrium**, which is disrupted by rebellions against conformism and restored through Lester's death, a most serene equilibrium. However, when you look closer, the film only appears to restore an equilibrium, which at the same time leaves all the major issues and characters unresolved.

- Most significantly, the issue of the potential effect of homophobia, and the repression in which it's rooted, is not resolved. Lester's death merely opens up that issue – just as the issue of all the different forms of social and psychological repression in the film are not answered by Lester's death. They can't be – they can only be confronted by audiences who are invited to reflect on them.

Lévi-Strauss: binary oppositions – only an apparent resolution of conflict?

• Look at these oppositions:

Positives	Negatives
Activity – prepared to act	Passivity
Rebellion	Acquiescence, acceptance, conformism
Opting out of such striving, ambition	American Dream – individual striving
Anti-materialism, spirituality	Materialism
Life	Death
Awareness of limitations	Unaware of limitations
Self-knowledge	Lack of self-knowledge
Prepared not to conform	Conformism
Inner beauty	American Beauty
Expression – sexuality – as therapeutic	Repression – repression of sexuality and sexual orientation harmful

• There is some kind of resolution of those opposites but in a provisional way. This suggests that resolution is neither achievable in reality nor in fiction.

• Ricky has a sense of beauty gained at the cost of considerable authoritarian, tyrannical oppression and financed by a dubious source of income.

• Ricky and Jane achieve some kind of liberation, even if a precarious one.

• Equally, Lester achieves some kind of resolution through death. Carolyn seems to gain tenuous resolution through the sense of awareness of what she has become. Angela, after moments of doubt, continues to reconstruct herself as the American Beauty.

• The major issue that oppression of whatever kind can have tragic consequences is exposed but not resolved.

Not the conventional narrative

It's all a puzzle. Yet the narrative does have a sense of closure, and it is arguably emotionally 'satisfying' for audiences. – i.e., there is a powerful emotional resolution. It is a narrative, however, which deliberately raises issues which demand thinking about rather than rapid resolution. The film's narrative draws attention to problems in society that audiences are being asked to confront.

Narrative: bringing it all together

I've tried to look at how the narrative of *American Beauty* creates meanings. I've focused on:

• how the narrative is constructed within scenes of *American Beauty*;

• how the different ways of considering narrative structure can be related to *American Beauty*.

3. Narrative and genre

Compare American Beauty's budget with films it competed with on its UK release:

Sleepy Hollow: *$65m*

Angela's Ashes: *$25m*

Stigmata: *$32m*

The Bone Collector: *$48m*

Which of the above are genre films? Check imdb.com

Both of these explorations lead to the main and most obvious function of a narrative: to please, entertain, involve and raise issues, i.e., generate responses as well as create meanings.

I've already suggested that it's probably not possible to interpret a narrative in one way. Narratives suggest several, often competing interpretations and those interpretations will depend on the different social and cultural backgrounds of audiences. That's why it's helpful to think in terms of possible interpretations rather than one single meaning of a film narrative. Nevertheless, you might recognise that there is a preferred or dominant interpretation, which represents the way the majority of people think.

American Beauty and genre

… kind of Sunset Boulevard *meets* Ordinary People *meets Paul Thomas Anderson meets* The Simpsons *meets* Happiness *meets* Election…?

Thinking about the genre – or possible genre – of a film is important for two reasons:

- it is a way of exploring how audiences relate to films and the reasons why audiences like films;

- it is a way of exploring how the film industry works to try and secure commercial success for films.

American Beauty is not a 'genre film'. It isn't in an easily recognisable genre like a sci-fi, horror, Western, comedy or crime film, to name some of the obvious genres. So be warned: *American Beauty* is not a very good film for exploring how mainstream genres work. It does, however, reveal a number of fascinating things about genre today – for

example, how the Hollywood industry uses genre and how we as audiences respond to films. It would thus provide an excellent means of exploring the significance of genre in film-making and film viewing today – compared with a mainstream genre film and an independent film, for example.

Checking *American Beauty*'s genre

Let's check the claim that *American Beauty* is not a 'genre film'. It does doubtless have elements of the crime, comedy, romance and even teen genre but it would be difficult to categorise as any one of those and most people (if pressed) would I think label it as 'drama'. The point about 'drama' is that it doesn't *seem* to function as a genre: audiences don't appear to think in terms of drama in the same way they do with science fiction and neither do Hollywood producers. In both cases that's probably because 'drama' doesn't have an easily understandable set of conventions, still less a history, which audiences and hence producers, would recognise. A further check you can do is pitch the film. Can you pitch *American Beauty* in terms of similar genre films?

Drama not a genre?

It might not be a precisely defined genre, but we all go into DVD/video shops and look at the drama section. It must mean something to us as audiences. And it does clearly mean something to DVD/video distributors, whose statistics by genre quote 'drama' as more popular than sci-fi and horror but less popular than comedies, thrillers and action films.

For the industry, 'drama' is perhaps too broad a category to predict audience reaction and base commercial decisions on.

The pitching game…

If you play the pitching game, as parodied by Robert Altman in his 1992 film, *The Player*, it's difficult to think of what you would come up with. Is *American Beauty* a kind of *Sunset Boulevard* meets *Ordinary People* meets Paul Thomas Anderson meets *The Simpsons* meets *Happiness* meets *Election* (1999)…? You may well have a better (or more preposterous) list. The point is, it's difficult to relate the film to predecessors and can't be sold either to producers or audiences in those terms.

Have a look at how Alan Ball pitched the ideas for the film in section 5 – he found it difficult but did not describe it either in terms of genre or actors.

Rental share by genre (2000)

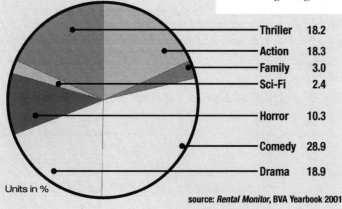

Genre	Units in %
Thriller	18.2
Action	18.3
Family	3.0
Sci-Fi	2.4
Horror	10.3
Comedy	28.9
Drama	18.9

Units in %

source: *Rental Monitor*, BVA Yearbook 2001

So this is a film without an obvious genre and which is difficult to relate to predecessors. However, *American Beauty* was both popular with audiences and did attract finance, admittedly only a lower than medium budget of $15m. A production budget of $15m puts *American Beauty* firmly outside the budget an average genre film would attract and is only mildly above what an independent feature would cost. I think this suggests several things about how genre is seen by audiences and the industry today and about the way *American Beauty* works with audiences. Let's think about audiences first.

A different take on genre - audiences

Genre films rely on repeating the familiar with some, even if slight, variations. In other words, audiences enjoy seeing the familiar but appear to enjoy even more the unexpected.

You might say that the whole of *American Beauty* challenges audiences' expectations. The narrative leads to one central shock: that the rabidly anti-gay Colonel Fitts – close to a stereotype of the right-wing military – is in fact a (repressed) homosexual. And that shock echoes the central idea of the film: that real beauty is where you'd least expect it – in the everyday, the familiar, the ordinary and the unconventional. It just depends on the way we look at things.

That major challenge to audience expectations is reflected throughout the film's narrative. You can see that when you think about the familiar elements in the narrative and the way each comes with some slight variation. Have a look at the following:

The familiar: what you'd expect	*Variations on the familiar: what you get in* American Beauty
Family – probably not nuclear, possibly a little dysfunctional	*Shows two families – one (the Fitts) considerably more dysfunctional than most*
Voiceover	*Not quite so common to have the voiceover coming from a dead person – but that famously does happen in* Sunset Blvd., *which the film overtly refers to*
Army colonel right-wing stereotype, anti-gay	*Repressed homosexual*
Teen school drama – central female characters	*Angela not what she seems and neither is Jane*
Affairs	*Resolved but not quite predictably*
Sets up enigma of how Lester will die – whether simply dies or is murdered or not - and why?	The reasons why Fitts murders Lester are not clear and not finally resolved (because spurned and humiliated, because of what Fitts thinks Lester stands for?)
Some questioning of hollowness of white middle-class suburban existence quite common	*Not straightforwardly film about pervy dad, right-wing fanatic, dysfunctional families, travesties of materialism, rebellious teens; but about need to value what you have, to see the beautiful in the ordinary*
Range of characters across generations: middle-aged dad fancying friend of younger daughter, wife having an affair, typical (individual and moody) adolescents. All familiar characters	*All characters not quite what they appear:* • *Lester: not the middle-age crisis lech but turns out to be sensitive to both Angela and Fitts* • *Carolyn: she too comes to recognise that people – Lester – is more important than 'stuff'* • *Ricky: not voyeur but observer, not exploitative drug-pusher but more benign supplier of recreational drugs?* • *Angela: more vulnerable than her sexually-experienced, vain persona suggests, virgin not sexually experienced* • *Jane: comes to recognise that an unconventional beauty is fine, that she is prepared to take control and liberate herself from domestic dysfunction* • *Fitts: not just right-wing stereotype but repressed homosexual*

3. Narrative and genre

You Know What You Are Going to Feel... reactions that rely on your familiarity with the horror genre

Each of the major elements of the narrative – from the characters to some of the digs at middle-class suburbia – is varied just a little more than we would expect. It suggests that audiences respond to the film because it plays against their expectations. And that's exactly what genre films do. They set up expectations that many audiences will recognise and provide variations on them. So *American Beauty* may not be a conventional genre film but it works for audiences in a very similar way. The central pleasures derived from genre films are perhaps common to all films which attract a broad and popular appeal.

Questioning genre

This raises several questions about genre. Rick Altman, in a book which itself calls into question several conventional ways of thinking about genre, claims this about films and genre:

> 'By definition, all films belong to some genre(s) but only certain films are self-consciously produced and consumed according to (or against) a specific generic model...when the notion of genre takes on a more active role in the production and consumption process, we appropriately speak instead of 'genre film', thus recognising the extent to which generic identification becomes a formative component of film viewing.'
>
> Altman, 1999

It's easy to see that a genre film is one where a familiarity with the genre is part of the way audiences relate to films – what Altman describes as a 'formative part of film viewing'. Watching a horror film like *I Know What You Did Last Summer* (1997) depends on (and plays with) your familiarity with the horror genre and slasher films in particular; so does the more recent *Cabin Fever* (2003). When he says that 'all films belong to some genre', perhaps he is suggesting that there are generic elements in all films. And this suggests that audiences can and do relate to films in ways which are outside the conventions of a specific genre but have reference to their knowledge of different generic conventions. Audience responses to *American Beauty* seem to support that by hinting that an important part of the film experience is relying on a pattern of measuring what we see against what we expect.

Another way of describing *American Beauty* is to say that it is a hybrid: it combines, for example, crime motifs (crime without detection, or even overt explanation for the murder – like John McNaughton's *Henry: Portrait of a Serial Killer* (1986) or Gus Van Sant's more recent *Elephant* (2003), which in more extreme form refuses to attempt to explain why the teenagers murdered the school students) with teenage angst and rebellion (plus romantic conclusion for Jane and Ricky) and portrays a distinctive kind of 'romance' between older man and younger girl, all with several comic (and tragic) touches.

In that sense, *American Beauty* is an example of the hybrid films Hollywood has been producing recently. Or perhaps hybrids aren't as recent a phenomenon as we might think. Musicals in the 40s after all combined romance, even melodrama, with the musical (*Meet Me In St Louis* (1944)) and science fiction films from at least the 1950s have frequently combined science fiction with horror (such as *The Thing* (1982) or *Alien* films (1979–1997)).

Richard Maltby (1995) might be right when he claims that it is critics (or DVD/video rental store managers?) who tend to cling to a rather fixed notion of genres rather than either producers or audiences, who are in essence much more flexible and thus more open to the idea of the hybrid:

> 'Critics place movies into generic categories as a way of dividing up the map of Hollywood cinema into smaller, more manageable, and relatively discrete areas... Audiences and producers use generic terms much more flexibly.'
>
> Richard Maltby (1995)

Even so, Hollywood – in keeping with a contemporary culture and society which is wedded to mixing and reusing – has emphasised and sold the idea of hybridity more in the last 20 years or so.

Putting this all together

To help you collect your own ideas on the issues underlying genre which *American Beauty* raises, you might look at the following claims made about genre.

---

testing out the theory: a few perspectives

- *Look for two films which support or question the claims below.*

- *How do the statements relate to* American Beauty*?*

- *For the slightly more difficult claims, there are some additional questions to give you some prompts.*

1: 'Simply stated, genre movies are those commercial feature films which, through repetition and variation, tell familiar stories with familiar characters.' (Barry Keith Grant, 1995)

2: 'Critics place movies into generic categories as a way of dividing up the map of Hollywood cinema into smaller, more manageable, and relatively discrete areas...Audiences and producers use generic terms much more flexibly.' (Richard Maltby, 1995)

3: 'Genre notions...are sets of cultural conventions. Genre is what we collectively believe it to be.' (Andrew Tudor, 1974)

- Andrew Tudor was referring to audiences when he talked in terms of 'we'. Are all audiences the same?

- What do you think he means by 'cultural conventions'?

4: [Genres are]...'systems of orientations, expectations and conventions that circulate between industry, text and subject.' Genres 'can function to provide, simultaneously, both regulation and variety.' (Steve Neale, 1980)

- What does 'circulating' between 'industry, text and subject' suggest? [Simple translation: 'Text' = film, 'subject' = audience]

5: 'By definition, all films belong to some genre(s) but only certain films are self-consciously produced and consumed according to (or against) a specific generic model. When the notion of genre is limited to descriptive uses, as it commonly is when serving classification purposes, we speak of "film genre". However, when the notion of genre takes on a more active role in the production and consumption process, we appropriately speak instead of "genre film", thus recognising the extent to which generic identification becomes a formative component of film viewing.' (Rick Altman, quoted in Steve Neale, 2000)

- How far do you agree with this statement?

- Does that mean we should only deal with 'genre films' in studying genre for A Level? Do we all agree on what is a 'genre film'?

6: 'Hollywood is a generic cinema, which is not quite the same as saying it is a cinema of genres.' (Richard Maltby, 1995)

7: 'Deliciously captured in Robert Altman's version of Michael Tolkin's screenplay *The Player*, Hollywood's basic script development practice involves (a) attempts to combine the commercial qualities of previously successful films, and (b) the consequent practice not only of mixing genres but of thinking about films in terms of the multiplicity of genres whose dedicated audiences they can attract.' (Rick Altman, 1999)

---

3. Narrative and genre

Rebel without a cause: originally a teen crime drama

© Warner Bros.

Holly (Sissy Spacek) and Kit (Martin Sheen) on the run in *Badlands*

Genre – the industry perspective

Those questions about genre necessarily take you into thinking about genre and the film industry. To restate the familiar as a start, genre is really inseparable from the development of the Hollywood film industry – although it is a feature of all major film industries, notably the world's largest film industry, India. Hollywood quickly realised that if audiences liked certain kinds of films, then commercial success could be guaranteed by providing more of the same. This led to Western films being made frequently at the same time and generally back-to-back in the Hollywood of the 1920s. Westerns were the most popular genre of the early Hollywood years, with 225 of them made in one year (1925).

Genre films minimise commercial risk by providing some way of estimating likely audience response. Since the time when the studio system was at its height, mainstream films have frequently been genre films and have been sold on that basis as a way of attracting audiences. Hence, commercial risk is minimised. As mentioned above, more recently Hollywood has tried to develop – or at least emphasise in their marketing – more hybrid genre films – mixing elements of several genres into the same film. You could think of *Blade Runner* (1982), *Pulp Fiction, The Matrix* (1999) or the *Alien* sequence of films.

American Beauty – not the producers' idea of a conventional genre film

We've already seen that for audiences, *American Beauty* was not thought of as a genre film. From Hollywood producers'

points of view, it was viewed as a 'character-driven story' (which was the way Dan Jinks, one of the film's producers, described *American Beauty*). That kind of film is characteristically worth a commercial risk – an investment of low to medium budget. However, the $15m invested in the film was low and presumably indicated some degree of speculation on DreamWorks' part. The film does incorporate hybrid elements – i.e., it would appeal to a reasonable cross-section of audiences – and does have a narrative, which mixes the familiar and the unexpected, as any genre film would be expected to do.

Interestingly, the original version of the script cast the whole film more overtly into the (teenage) crime drama mould, picking up on such films as Terrence Malick's *Badlands* (1973) and Oliver Stone's media parody, *Natural Born Killers* (1994) or *Kalifornia* (1993). It was originally framed by courtroom scenes, where Ricky and Jane were being tried for the murder of Lester Burnham and the main narrative effectively proved them innocent.

'The movie you see is not the movie I thought I was shooting. I thought I was making a much more whimsical, comic story, kaleidoscopic, almost like a Coen Brothers movie – *The Big Lebowski*, for example. Not to say that's what I was trying to make but I thought the tone was closer to that of whimsy. And what I found in the cutting-room, what I was instinctively drawn towards, was a much more emotional story. The darkness was always there, but I brought it into the movie much earlier: using Tom Newman's score, using certain shots I didn't think I'd use – or not at the length I used them.'

Sam Mendes, in Strick (2000)

NOTES:

Perhaps this is how Hollywood works at the lower to medium budget end of the film market. Films don't have to be mainstream genre films or even hybrid genre films to achieve commercial success; but they do have to refer to generic features and have strong narratives, which mix the familiar and the unexpected. It seems to be decision-making which does balance the economic interests of producers with audience interests – which is what 'genre' and 'generic features' arguably do.

American Beauty as a studio independent film?

Films which appear to work outside the conventions of identifiable genres are often associated with independent film-makers. That is itself a reflection of the fact that genre films are frequently opposed to films which represent the 'vision' of the director – where directors take the role of an auteur. (I'll be talking more about this in section 7.)

At face value *American Beauty* has all the hallmarks of an independent film and one strongly driven by its director, Sam Mendes. Interestingly, Jeffrey Sconce, an American critic, has suggested (2002) that American independent cinema has recently been producing films which are 'smart' and appears to be suggesting that for an art-house audience they almost function as a genre. One of the things they appear to have in common is that they question and challenge the American Dream. He lists films like these:

* *Grand Canyon* (1991)
* *The Ice Storm* (1997)
* *Bulworth* (1998)
* *Happiness* (1998)
* *Election* (1999)
* *Fight Club* (1999)
* *The Virgin Suicides* (1999).

This raises an interesting issue: do these films function a little like a sub-genre, a micro-climate of genre, attractive to film distributors and audiences alike because they share similar features?

A different take on genre – studio 'independents'?

The other thing that the above films (with the exception of *Happiness*) have in common is that they are all financed by Hollywood studios. They may be art-house films but they are not strictly 'independent' in the sense of being independent from Hollywood studios. 'Independent' is a relative term: it implies independence *from* something. In film terms, it has tended to mean produced, and thus financed, independently from the mainstream, Hollywood film industry.

Financial independence brought the freedom to control your film and that meant independent films tended to take more risks and be experimental. They were experimental either in terms of subject matter – through the issues the film raised and its narrative - or in terms of style (experimental camerawork, editing, mise-en-scène, sound). Films like Jim Jarmusch's *Stranger than Paradise* (1983) and *Mystery Train* (1989) from the 1980s or Kevin Smith's 1994 *Clerks* would be classic US examples.

More recently – as with the music and television industry, themselves owned by the same major media conglomerates – the distinction between mainstream studio production and independent production has been blurred. All the major studios have production and distribution companies which specialise in the 'art house', 'independent'-looking film market. Or when they haven't created a separate company, they divide their investments between the mainstream and art-house markets.

Hollywood has in other words found niche markets and has recognised that profits can be made through catering for a single mass market as well as more specialised markets. In some cases, there's even more profit in films which achieve commercial success on low to minimal investment. *The Full Monty*, distributed through Fox Searchlight, is an excellent example as it holds the record for the most profitable film, based on the ratio of its production and distribution budget to its overall profit.

Budgets

20th Century Fox
Grand Canyon: *$33m*
Bulworth: *$30m*
Fight Club: *$63m*

Fox Searchlight
The Ice Storm: *$18m*

Paramount/MTV
Election: *$8.5m*

Paramount Classics/Pathe:
The Virgin Suicides: *$6m*

Good Machine (independent):
Happiness: *$3m*
Stranger Than Paradise: *$90,000*
Mystery Train: *$367,000*
Clerks: *$27,000 (but a further $203,000 in post-production)*

Happiness: (relatively) low budget independent

The Virgin Suicides: studio independent

3. Narrative and genre

Parent Company (Hollywood Studio)	Company specialising in art-house production
News Corporation (20th Century Fox)	Fox Searchlight *The Full Monty* (1997), *The Ice Storm*
AOL Time Warner (Warner Bros)	New Line, Fine Line, HBO Gus Van Sant's *Elephant* (HB0)
Sony (Columbia Tristar)	Sony Picture Classics Tom De Cillo's *Living in Oblivion* (1995)
Disney (Buena Vista, Touchstone)	Miramax *Shakespeare in Love* (1998), *Chicago* (2002)
Paramount	Paramount Classics *The Virgin Suicides*

Niche market:

a specialised, smaller market, like the market for 'art house' films

'...[for independent films] there are certain marketing hooks...Those are: sex, food, music – and I mean classical music...'

Jeff Lipsky, marketing director, Samuel Goldwyn, quoted in Rob Feld's 'The Indie Film's Identity Crisis', Written By, Dec/Jan 2000

The English Patient: a crossover from the art house market to the mainstream

The Sundance Film Festival, originally established by Robert Redford as a showcase for independent films, which could then be sold to distributors, is an interesting indication of this shift. In the early 1990s few of the films on show would have had any distributor. Now, nearly all the films have distributors and Sundance is seen by the industry as more of a marketing opportunity, a prestigious showcase to launch a film.

What all this suggests is that the Hollywood film industry does have a broad view of genre. It uses genre as a starting point for its mainstream 'high concept' films – its blockbusters – which seem to have 'hybrid' features to ensure the maximum possible audience. But it is also prepared to think of art-house films (to be marketed as 'independent' films) as a separate category.

Jack Lechner, formerly at Miramax, commented at the time of *American Beauty*'s

release that the best independent films were now being made by studios and cited David O Russell's *Three Kings* (1999, Warner Bros), Alexander Payne's *Election* (Paramount) and David Fincher's *Fight Club* (20th Century Fox) as examples.

The dream that *American Beauty* fulfilled was that it started as a promising character-driven story, with independent features, and finished up by becoming a mainstream success. It was a crossover film – a film, like Anthony Minghella's *The English Patient* (1995) previously, which 'crossed over' from the independent, art house market to the mainstream. Its commercial success – the scale of which was however surprising – suggests that Hollywood no longer relies on genre as the only guide to commercial viability.

NOTES:

Narrative and genre – Worksheet 1

What do narratives suggest?  **Task**

Narratives create meanings for audiences.

- What does *American Beauty*'s narrative suggest?
- Does it suggest the same to you as it does to other audiences?
- What are *American Beauty*'s messages and values?
- What ideologies does it reinforce or challenge?

Approaching the task

First thoughts:

1. Ask questions about the title

How does the title relate to the various narrative elements in the film?
What are the connotations of the title?

Think about these connections:

- The rose, a seductive but ultimately superficial beauty ('American Beauty', the name of the rose hybrid)?

- An ideal female beauty, cherished by American society – represented most obviously by Angela, but also Carolyn? A beauty which relies on superficial image rather than emotional depth?

- the superficial material beauty striven for by those seeking the American Dream of material wealth and social status (superficial, illusory beauty of American Dream – a 'dream' just as 'fantastic' as Lester's fantasies of Angela)?

- The superficial gains of individual ambition – striving for the wrong things?

- Beauty found not in the obvious but in the less obvious?

- Are we conditioned to see beauty in the conventional? Do we need to be challenged to find beauty in the unconventional?

- Is the real beauty behind the 'American Beauty' a spiritual, mystical or inner beauty? Does the film suggest that individuals need to see past the superficial beauties of life – the apparently seductively beautiful women, materialism – to recognise the genuinely beautiful?

- Is beauty the 'entire life behind things' (Alan Ball)?

2. Look for scenes which support your interpretation

- Show how the micro and macro features in those scenes underline your interpretation

- Look to see what others have said: research on the web, film magazines and articles…

Narrative and genre – Worksheet 1.1

Research further

- Select key sentences and phrases from articles you've read.
- Make a list of ideas they suggest to you.
- Identify key scenes which support your views.

Phillip French [On Ricky]: 'The mystic heir to William Blake and Walt Whitman, he can see the wondrousness of life itself in a plastic bag being blown in the wind.' (Observer, 30 Jan 2000)

Philip Kemp 'The worm in the well-manicured bud of suburban life, the fears and loathings and sexual lacerations that lurk behind the white picket fence – these are no new subject for American cinema.' (Sight & Sound, Jan 2000)

Philip French 'Mendes manages to give individuality and distinction to some extremely familiar material.' (Observer, 30 Jan 2000).

Sam Mendes '…the camera's impassive and uninflected gaze.'

Glen Kenny '…the final evocation of grace among ruins is both haunting and heartening.'

Alan Ball One of the movie' themes is how we have preconceived notions about things, but the truth often turns out to be something we never even considered – where you find true beauty might be in the place you least expect it.'

Alan Ball '[What happens to Lester] is not so much mid-life crisis, but rather a sort of rebirth. He comes to realise how precious life is…a realisation that's in some ways too late.'

Eve MacSweeney 'The interior world that lurks beneath the surface of our lives is a major theme of American Beauty.'

Andrew Gumbel Both Fight Club and American Beauty in their different ways are films about emasculation – the withering sense of male powerlessness in the modern world…'

Narrative and genre – Worksheet 1.2

Test out your ideas with this interpretation of
American Beauty

- Highlight statements you agree with and those you don't
- Select short extracts from the film to support your views.

American Beauty is about individuals' need to challenge the pressures which force them to conform to a conventional life. Through that challenge, they gain some kind of recognition of what's most important to them.

Lester rebels against the banality and futility of his daily existence, both at work (working as a media sales person, an image of promoting the superficial) and at home. The catalyst is his desire to be sexually attractive to Angela. He comes to recognise that what's important is what is closest to him – his family.

Carolyn equally tries to assert her individuality – liberating herself through an affair. Her recognition equally comes too late – appalling pathos of closet wardrobe scene.

Ricky and Jane assert themselves to achieve their independence.

- Fitts is unable to confront his own repressed sexuality, or the pressures which lead him to deny it, with tragic consequences.

Because the world is round it turns me on
Because the world is round...aaaaaaaabhhh

Because the wind is high it blows my mind
Because the wind is high...aaaaaaaabhhh

Love is all, love is new
Love is all, love is you

Because the sky is blue, it makes me cry
Because the sky is blue, ...aaaaaaaabhhh

Aaaaaaaabhhh...

(*Because*, Lennon.McCartney, 1969)

Narrative and genre – Worksheet 2

Questions about genre:

Genre is a 'kind' or 'type' of film, like science fiction or horror. It's a way of categorising films. We recognise also that genres are dynamic and flexible – they are constantly open to change. Genres thus change historically and often become ways of raising and addressing issues in an accessible way.

The significance of genre

The Matrix Reloaded: *How far are* The Matrix *films sci-fi and marketed as such? Do audiences respond to them as sci-fi films?*

- Who does the categorising? Is it the industry (producers, distributors and exhibitors), who believe that labels sell and help make it easy to attract audiences to films? Or do audiences actually dictate what is thought of as a genre, through attending them? Lots of 'sub-genres' seem to be like that. At what point does a serial killer or a teen film become a genre that audiences think of a separate genre?

- Do audiences categorise films in the same way as the industry and does it matter? Perhaps audiences are very happy to think of 'drama' as a genre – if that means something to most audiences?

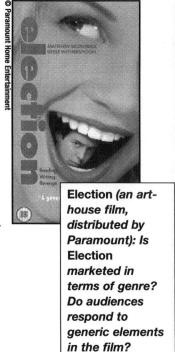

Election (*an art-house film, distributed by Paramount*): *Is* Election *marketed in terms of genre? Do audiences respond to generic elements in the film?*

The underlying assumption is that genres are familiar and as audiences we like the familiar: the enjoyment of seeing a genre film often comes down to getting what we expect but also seeing slight variations from completely formulaic repetitions. Genres thus combine the repetition and variation of conventions.

- Audiences seem to assimilate conventions almost unconsciously. Why do people enjoy seeing familiar things repeated? Is it the pleasure of fulfilling expectations which lead to emotional satisfaction?

Narrative and genre – Worksheet 3

Popular along with *American Beauty*

These are the top three grossing films from the major Hollywood studios in 1999. How many are genre films?

Studio	Top 3 grossing films in 1999
Paramount	*Runaway Bride* *Double Jeopardy* *The General's Daughter*
Sony	*Big Daddy* *Stuart Little* *Blue Streak*
20th Century Fox	*Star Wars Episode 1 – The Phantom Menace* *Entrapment* *Never Been Kissed*
Universal	*The Mummy* *Notting Hill* *American Pie*
Warner Bros	*The Matrix* *The Wild* *Wild West* *Analyze This*
Disney	*The Sixth Sense* *Toy Story 2* *Tarzan*
MGM/UA	*The World Is Not Enough* *The Thomas Crown Affair* *Stigmata*
DreamWorks	*The Haunting* *American Beauty* *Forces of Nature*

Always on their minds...

Jack Lechner on genre and producers again:

'**"One of the smartest things that Harvey [Weinstein, at Miramax] always did...was to look at what people are not doing now. What are the genres that no one has done in a long time that you can breathe new life back into."** He mentions Scream (1996) as a classic Miramax example of this.'*

(in Rob Feld's 'The Indie Film's Identity Crisis', Written By, Dec/Jan 2000)

Narrative and genre – Worksheet 4

Exploring the macro features of American Beauty –
narrative and genre

How do narratives create meanings and generate response?

Approaching the task

Getting an overview
- Start with the title and its connotations.

Choosing the sequence
- Choose a series of scenes which seem to highlight the main issues the film raises.
- Choose a sequence of scenes you particularly like – where you can see the narrative unfolding.

Exploring the sequence
- Explore how the scene is constructed – how does it tell a story?
- Focus on:
  - the role of editing…juxtaposition of shots to create meaning, length of shot, what kinds of cutting are used, how editing reveals character;
  - how the scene suggests ideas and raises issues through the connotations of individual shots and through visual referencing (intertextuality and parallelism);
  - how the narrative involves the audience;
  - how it plays on assumptions audiences make and raise expectations;
  - how it positions audiences and suggests points of view about what is seen on screen.
- Explore narration and point of view and how that affects narrative.

Using the theories
It is generally better to develop a close analysis of how narratives create meanings and how they position audiences before considering theoretical perspectives.

If you choose to use a theoretical perspective, other more specific questions to explore narrative and narrative structure might be:

- What is the role of editing in generating audience response within a short narrative sequence?
- How are meanings built up through the juxtaposition of different storylines within a narrative sequence?
- How are meanings created through visual references to other moments in the film and through intertextuality in a narrative sequence you have explored?
- How far is equilibrium restored in the final sequence of the film?
- How are characters established and enigmas created in the opening of your film?

More demanding questions

- Use a particular sequence to explore how far you think the narrative positions audiences.
- Explore how far you think your chosen sequence suggests it's being narrated from a particular point of view.
- How does a narrative sequence reinforce audience beliefs in the nature of cause and effect and of the rational explanation of people's behaviour?
- How far does the film's ending resolve the binary opposites of the film in a way which they don't in real life?
- How far does the ending of your film reinforce dominant ideologies of society today?

Narrative and genre – Worksheet 4.1

How do generic elements generate response and create meanings?

Note: Exploring how genre relates to American Beauty *is a challenging task, precisely because it is not a mainstream genre film in an ordinary sense. It is probably not a suitable film for exploring mainstream genres.*

Challenging questions

• Explore how generic conventions from a range of films are used in a sequence from *American Beauty*.

• Explore how one sequence from American Beauty shares characteristics common to contemporary genre films.

For more conventional genre films and their hybrids

• Identify the standard conventions of your chosen film's genre and show how they are used in a sequence of your choice.

• Explore how conventional the opening/ conclusion of your chosen film is.

• Show how a sequence from your chosen film repeats and varies the conventions of its genre.

• Show how audience expectations are fulfilled and/or challenged in a sequence of your choice.

4. Representations and the real

Gender and sex

There is technically a distinction between the biological bases which distinguish men from women – sex differences – and gender, which describes the patterns of behaviour, thinking and feeling associated with men and women. This suggests that gender is like a role which people gradually adopt. It is, as psychologists put it, learned behaviour. One of the main ways people learn roles is through films and the media.

The naïve look of delight as Barbara Fitts offers cooked breakfast to her son

Burbank sets

Amongst many other films, the Fitts' house was used in the Lethal Weapon *(1987–1998) series of films and the Burnham's house was used in* Divorce American Style *(1967), which Conrad Hall himself filmed some 30 years earlier.*

At the root of all film and media studies is a fundamental issue: that most films (as well as all forms of media, including television) often look as if they provide a window on reality. We tend to forget that what we see is actually something *constructed* to look as if it were a window on the real world. Everything about films is made to convince us that what we are looking at is real. Sets and locations, characters and how they act, lighting and narratives are all designed to convey a sense of reality which audiences think is 'like real life'. What film-makers are actually doing, however, is constructing films and providing their version of reality.

Representations

You could say that films are *constructed* in two senses. First, we all know that much of what we see in films is a constructed set. In *American Beauty*, the houses on Robin Hood Drive, in 'affluent, suburban Connecticut' (screenplay directions) were in fact old sets used in several television series on the Warner Burbank studios site (and apparently suffered from rat infestation). Second, what we see is *constructed* in a more metaphorical sense. It's a construction of the film-makers' version of the real world. What we see is therefore not how people and societies actually are but how the film-makers see those people and societies and encourage us to see them. So importantly, film-makers are never simply showing, they are showing us people and the world we live in with points of view about them.

You could therefore say that what we see on screens are images plus points of view about those images. A formal way of expressing that is to say we see ideological representations. The reason why it's so important to ask questions about how people and issues are represented in films is that they seem to shape the way we all think and feel. I'd like to explore how gender, sexual orientation, family, race and issues such as materialism and the American Dream are represented in *American Beauty* in order to consider these points.

Gender: representation of women

Let's start by asking a few questions about some individual female characters and ask whether the way they are portrayed in *American Beauty* is beginning to suggest to audiences ways in which women think, feel, act and behave in society. I've already looked at how Carolyn is portrayed (in section 2). I'd like now to look at Barbara Fitts.

Three key scenes where she appears are in the kitchen preparing breakfast, the dining room and the final scene where Ricky leaves. Is there anything common in the way she's portrayed in these scenes? You might come up with the following:

- she's not actually named in the film – the credits tell you she's called Barbara Fitts;

- the dialogue she speaks is minimal;

- her facial expressions are almost all a mixture of blank and harrowed – there's a slight, naïve look of delight as she cooks bacon for Ricky, only to find that her maternal role is here irrelevant (as he doesn't eat bacon);

- her behaviour suggests something between being absent-minded and psychologically damaged;

- she doesn't initiate any conversation, either with her husband or her son;

- there seems a steady decline between the way we first see her and the way Ricky leaves her;

- a key scene is where we see her sitting vacantly at the end of a highly polished table in the dining room, being introduced to Jane in a way which suggests she has a weak grip on her sanity.

Having got an overall impression of how she is portrayed, look more carefully at how she is presented cinematically in the dining room scene I've just referred to. What is the point of view being conveyed about her?

<table>
<tr><td>

A checklist for analysing still images and key scenes

Image...
- What do you literally see (the denotations of the image)?

- What does that suggest (the connotations of the image)?

...plus point of view
- What is being suggested by the image – effectively, what point of view is being conveyed about the image?

How is that point of view conveyed? What role do the following micro features play?

- framing, position of camera in relation to action

- mise-en-scène (sets, lighting, dress in particular)

- camerawork (distance, angle, movement)

- editing (what's selected, length of shot, what's it juxtaposed with, manipulated in any way?)

- anchorage (script/dialogue, voiceover narration)

How do macro features foreground points of view?

- issues raised, how scenes are structured and juxtaposed with one another, narrative enigmas and tensions, how they are resolved

- what role does genre or generic features play (where relevant – less so in this particular film – see section 3)?

</td></tr>
</table>

Ideology

- *set of attitudes, values and beliefs*

- *because people have particular attitudes, beliefs and values they see the world in particular ways*

- *ideology could thus be described as a 'way of seeing the world'.*

Denotations
- You might see the fixed, emotionless, vacant expression, the slightly greying hair, the immaculate but conservatively dark tones of the room, the reflection of the image on the table, the perfectly symmetrical framing, the clock ticking.

Emotionless expression, emotional emptiness

Connotations
- The connotations of the image are of an emotional emptiness, more exaggerated than the earlier dining room scene at the Burnhams. And further, they convey a joylessness, a person cowered into some kind of emotional or psychological numbness. How does this compare with Lester's description of himself as being dead already? All she can do is clean everything so that the table reflects her image – Barbara Fitts is no more than a reflection of herself.

Those are the connotations of the image, then. How are they underlined cinematically?

4. Representations and the real

Cinematic presentation: conveying and underlining representations

framing & mise-en-scène

- key shot - medium long shot, slight tilt (higher angle) exploiting depth of focus, symmetrical composition, Barbara Fitts, with immaculately polished table in front of her, in centre of frame – vacant, lifeless expression;

- the emptiness of mise-en-scène underlines the empty and controlled Barbara Fitts.

Camerawork

- 90°, slight tilt shot, looking down on Barbara Fitts, emphasised by Ricky's leaning down to speak with her – underlining the sympathy audiences are invited to feel.

sound

- shift from reflective sound of street and talk of death to the hollow, clock ticking, emphasising lifelessness (and time passing?) inside house.

editing & narrative structure

- length of shots on mother – sense of lingering, with little camera movement, again to emphasise the lifelessness of the scene;

- juxtaposition with previous scene (suggestive discussion of a frozen, homeless, dead woman, as though hinting that Barbara Fitts is as if frozen, dead & alienated in her own home);

- cut to following shot of close-ups on guns and medium shots of Fitts' concealed and locked room, suggestive of what is psychologically hidden and what fuels the dominance he exerts over wife and household.

Uncovering the points of view

When the scene continues, it's almost painful to see how gently Ricky introduces Jane, knowing that his mother is absent-minded. There's a delayed reaction before she breaks into a mechanical smile; and what does she say? She apologises for the way things look.

Responses to patriachal oppression?

This is interestingly ironic: you first of all think, perhaps like Jane, that the woman is forced into her daily routine of obsessive cleaning by Colonel Fitts. It's as though he demands a military orderliness around the home. It thus becomes an image of his control over her – of the way he has sucked the life out of her. But perhaps there is also a sense in which she realises what her home looks like? From that point of view, she is apologising for the way things look – dead, cold and emotionally sterile. It makes the scene even more painful.

The scene is further punctuated by the *editing* and narrative structure, as suggested above. We shift from talk of a homeless woman who had frozen to death to Fitts' concealed and locked room, suggesting the way Fitts freezes his wife and household by his controlling personality.

The point of view

What point of view is thus being conveyed by this portrayal of Barbara Fitts? Does the scene raise questions about the role of women in today's society? One of the issues underlying the significance of representations is that there is a tendency for audiences to relate the individual to the group. Audiences might not see just one individual woman but will respond to what that woman's experience suggests about women in today's society. In many ways, films provide a narrative world with several people in it who give an impression of what it's like to be a woman in today's society. Barbara Fitts and the other female characters in the film are representations of different kinds of female experience in today's society. They suggest an ideological representation of women — a portrayal of women with the film-makers' points of view about them, which we as audiences will debate.

NOTES:

Points of view about Barbara and Carolyn – the roots of an ideological representation

Barbara Fitts:

- dominated by Fitts, she is an image of a subjugated woman, incapable of challenging Fitts' patriarchal attitudes;

- she is repressed and withdrawn (to the point of psychological imbalance);

- all emotions, sexual or otherwise, are sublimated in an excessive domesticity.

Carolyn Burnham:

- apparently domineering, she is arguably the image of a woman who is assertive, determined and independent;

- underlying that assertiveness, however, is a fragility and vulnerability;

- all her emotions, sexual or otherwise, are sublimated in the excessive tending of her garden (and roses) and the furnishing of the house.

With Barbara we see a disturbing result of male dominance – an image of patriarchal elements in society today; with Carolyn, we begin to see that she is assertive because she is challenging the competitive male world of real estate business. She is modelling success on a version of the ambitiousness which is associated with competitiveness and men. The film represents both as needing to liberate themselves from the different kinds of oppressive attitudes they have assimilated. One of the several disturbing elements of the film is the way it doesn't resolve any of these narrative or representational issues: Carolyn's attempts to liberate herself are represented as grotesque (although there is a sense of recognising the circumstances she's created as she crumbles in front of the bedroom wardrobe at the end of the film); and Barbara Fitts is left in that haunting image of vacancy and acceptance as Ricky leaves her.

Jane and Angela

The complementary images of women suggested by Barbara and Carolyn are echoed in Jane and Angela. Jane's desires to be more attractive (to get her breasts enlarged) appears to be a response to the prevalent stereotypical male attitudes of female beauty she has assimilated – and which Ricky will enable her to challenge. Angela's aspirations to become a model example of 'American Beauty' (in all senses) are again founded on a male view of superficial, sexual attraction. Cinematically, lighting and camerawork often accentuates this difference. Angela is generally lit more glamorously than Jane (as in the first occasion when Lester meets Angela after the basketball game) but camera shots search out the individual beauty of Jane – such as the over-the-shoulder close-ups of Jane when Ricky first introduces himself in the school grounds.

All the women are represented as responding differently to patriarchal attitudes, ranging from the dominated to the challenging:

- Barbara Fitts – conforming to the role assigned to her by men's values to the point of complete subjugation;

- Angela – conforming to men's idea of women's sexuality;

- Carolyn – having to assert herself in an apparently male-oriented business and adopting the competitive, aggressive values associated with men;

- Jane – on the point of being subservient to men's images of women, she challenges that pressure to conform.

The representation is thus ideological: it is a representation with a point of view which audiences are invited to respond to.

Gender: representation of men

To sharpen this focus, you could ask several questions about how men and masculinity are represented in the film. To gain an overview, think about the representational issues five key scenes bring up in narrative terms:

Key scenes to explore representation of Jane

Jane & Angela in the car after basketball game.

Jane with Ricky in his room, when they video each other.

Final scenes – Ricky going off with Jane, confronting Angela and Angela with Lester.

4. Representations and the real

Exploring representations

Always ask how micro and macro features underline representations.

Representations of men

Conrad Hall made the suggestion to use handheld cameras in this scene.

Sam Mendes and Conrad Hall talk about this scene on the DVD discussion of the storyboard.

Lester is shot from high angles in many of these opening scenes to portray his low status and powerlessness.

- Lester and Carolyn in bed (his fantasies of Angela and confronting his wife);

- Fitts beating up Ricky;

- Fitts and the two Jims;

- Ricky walking home with Jane;

- climactic scene with Fitts and Lester.

In the same way that the central female characters come to represent different responses to what is portrayed as a male-oriented society, the male characters are shown in a similar context. The scenes might suggest the following:

- Fitts is represented as controlling, domineering, potentially aggressive and violent – a representation suggestive of repression;

- Lester is represented as an average male, with average sexual desires (with familiar, even stereotypical, mid-life fantasies about younger women) but fundamentally sensitive and not aggressive;

- Ricky is portrayed as secure and mature but, like Jane, the most able person to challenge and liberate himself from the main agent of oppression – his father;

- the Jims' sexual orientation is represented as not an issue – and arguably they are represented as the least repressed and dysfunctional characters in the film's narrative (see comments on 'sexual orientation' below).

Underlying these basic issues is again a sense of patriarchal attitudes – Fitts' oppressive, authoritarian dominance, the competitive corporate environment of Lester's work, full of hypocrisy – which to varying degrees entail repression, which

each male figure attempts to confront in some way. It's only Ricky who finally succeeds in freeing himself from those patriarchal attitudes – through his perceptions of seeing beyond the superficial and his eventual escape from his parents' home.

A slightly more detailed exploration of scenes supports these views.

Fitts

Fitts is the character who portrays in the most extreme form oppressive, authoritarian and thus patriarchal views. In the early kitchen scene, his control over his wife and family is already apparent in the framing and *mise-en-scène*, where the attention is drawn to Fitts' reading the paper. The length of the shots prior to him answering the door accentuates that he dictates action in the household. And his views about gay sexuality are made effortlessly clear in the scene which follows (see below). His later resort to the most extreme violence with his son – based on his own perceptions of what he thinks he has seen – betrays the pent-up aggression he has. The extremity of this violence is underlined by the fast cutting and the handheld camerawork, the only moment in the film where handheld cameras are used – which makes the scene even more conspicuous. The oppression he exerts over his family is exposed as hypocritical: he is himself repressing his own gay, sexual orientation. And that of course has disastrous, tragic consequences.

Lester

Look again at the early two scenes: Lester is established as being dominated by – even emasculated and subjugated by - the women in his family ('Both my wife and daughter think I'm this gigantic loser,

NOTES:

and...they're right') and to a monotonous job which doesn't bring status, importance or any kind of self-fulfilment. The camerawork in particular emphasises that: the shot, reverse shot along the 180° line of the scene where he drops his case followed by the scowling, dismissive look of Carolyn (higher/lower angle again accentuates that power). Similarly at work, the distance between Brad as interviewer and Lester as interviewee is exaggerated by open body language, camerawork and mise-en-scène to show him as powerless. Sam Mendes indeed adds that as audiences we laugh just a little more at the way his pencil has the football eraser on its end. The two scenes together represent men as pressurised into conformity in the home and at work. But note how in both cases, the world of home and work are both associated with patriarchal values – the competitive, materialistic values of American society.

Lester's own sense of himself as a man is thus framed by the dual pressures of home and work: Carolyn's middle-class materialism and determination to succeed (a control suggested by the mise-en-scène – the cold décor of the home and the 'elevator music' which are both hers). Compared with Carolyn, he is represented as useless. At work, we sense that he's not even prepared to play the game – not even able to recognise the need to succeed. He is trapped and repressed.

His mid-life crisis of masculinity – doubtless familiar, even stereotypical – actually becomes the means by which he is able to liberate himself and come to recognise the value of what he has had all along – his family. Ironically, that comes through the crush he develops for his daughter's best friend.

Ricky

Ricky is portrayed as not only sensitive, confident and mature – the one person who can see the beauty in the less obvious – but also as the one figure who successfully challenges conformity and his oppressively authoritarian father. However, his whole ability to see – to record what he observes – is financed through drugs (represented without censure – almost as if recreational drugs were also a means by which people can exercise independence from everyday conformity). So with Jane, he's represented as a person who's open, prepared to look and be looked at, who sees beyond a superficial, male-oriented sexuality and opts out of conformism. He is capable of conforming but in a way which registers his

control over the pressures to conform – he can simulate conformity with his father's insidious oppressive, reactionary views. (You might think of the car scene with his father, where he exaggeratedly parodies an anti-gay attitude).

Gender representation

When you put the representations of women and men together, they both seem to be defined in terms of a reference to patriarchal attitudes. Underlying all the representations of women and men is the ideological view that conformity to the patriarchal values underlying contemporary society is repressive. In different ways, women and men attempt to break free from those pressures. That freedom, however, comes at a cost. The values which emerge are that personal expression is crucial and that pressures to conform should be challenged. All authority is portrayed as oppressive and suffocates individuality and independence.

Sexual orientation

The two Jims are represented first of all as neighbours and secondly as gay. Their gay sexuality isn't hidden – it's even portrayed humorously, via the reference to the dog and its jerky treat, for example, but in an accepting way. We're not being positioned to laugh at them any more than at Carolyn. Lester, in his opening voiceover, also introduces them with humour. 'That's our next-door neighbour, Jim...And that's his lover, Jim.'

When they both call to welcome Fitts their neighbour, the social acceptability of gay sexuality is emphasised through Fitts' excessive and, as we later find out, repressed reactions. The same shots are used to allow audiences to respond to the dialogue and what it reveals: medium shots, slightly angled against the 180° line, allow audiences to capture the Jims' expressions as they point out what each 'partner' does and reverses to Fitts on whom the shot is held as it gradually 'dawns on him' (script directions) and allows the audience to savour the humour and thus position themselves with the two Jims. Audiences are further positioned to accept gay sexuality by laughing at Fitts' reactions in the next shot at the same time as finding them disturbing. The

Ricky – the sensitive male and the one person who can see beauty in the everyday

4. Representations and the real

Audience positioning: acceptance of gay sexuality

Editing positions audiences first of all to laugh at Fitts and therefore recognise how extreme his point of view is.

1: MS of two Jims capturing their facial expressions as they explain what each 'partner' does.

2: MS held on Fitts for his gradual recognition of what they mean by 'partner'.

3: Side angle MS held on Fitts and otherwise occupied Ricky (calculating his drugs profits).

'They don't feel like it's anything to be ashamed of.'

4: Side angle CU of Ricky:

'...those fags make me want to puke my fucking guts out.'

juxtaposition of these two scenes shows clearly the effect of editing to underline an issue. The side angle, medium shot, is held as Fitts and Ricky exchange views:

COLONEL How come these faggots always have to rub it in your face? How can they be so shameless?

RICKY That's the whole thing, Dad. They don't feel like it's anything to be ashamed of.

The camerawork cuts to side angle close-ups as Ricky ends up mechanistically reciting what he thinks his father expects him to feel:

RICKY Forgive me, sir, for speaking so bluntly, but those fags make me want to puke my fucking guts out.

Audiences are being positioned to find this funny – the reverse reaction shots at the end of the scene, showing Fitts bemused but finally agreeing – as well as unsavoury and excessive.

This scene is part of the narrative's construction of Fitts as repressive and repressed. The narrative reveals gradually his attitudes and feelings, culminating in the climactic scene in the garage with Lester. Audiences are encouraged to recognise in this scene that Fitts' feelings towards gay sexuality are more than merely prejudicial. His subsequent (incorrect) suspicions about Lester's sexual orientation are conveyed when we see him associating Lester with the two Jims on the morning run. This fuels the way the audience sees him look at Ricky's footage of the bare-chested Lester lifting weights in the garage (not initially portrayed as voyeuristic) and his misinterpretation of the scene between Ricky and Lester. The violence of his verbal and physical reactions invites audiences to sense that such reactions are not conventional. Nevertheless, the savage attack on Ricky (underlined by the only example of handheld camerawork in the film) is initially represented to audiences as the violent reaction of a militaristic parent, appalled at his son's behaviour (as he interprets it).

Fitts is thus represented as repressed and becomes an emblem of the consequences of repressing and denying feelings as well as of not confronting prejudicial feelings in general.

Representation of family

The representation of family in the film is similarly rooted in changes in our understanding of what constitutes family life; rarely do we see entirely happy nuclear families at the centre of contemporary films. This is not to say, however, that families are necessarily defined negatively. *The Simpsons* and several films which do portray families – like Sam Mendes' *Road to Perdition* – still imply that the values emanating from families – whether they are conventional nuclear families or not – remain important. *American Beauty*, however, initially represents the family as corrosive. Dysfunction equates to oppression.

Test this out by looking at some of the significant scenes in film:

- the Fitts' watching television: Mother, Father and Ricky – Ronald Reagan extract – parody of father;

- the early morning kitchen scene at the Fitts';

- the several scenes showing the relationship between Fitts and Ricky, culminating in his violence towards Ricky;

- the first dinner table scene at the Burnhams, followed by Lester's attempting to talk with Jane;

- Carolyn and Jane's confrontation (the 'Kodak moment').

Both homes' décor suggests different kinds of oppressive coldness: the Burnhams' is indicative of cold control, the Fitts' a sublimated expression of Barbara Fitts' response to her husband's controlling presence. Both are oppressive. Oppressed by middle-class materialism, their aspirations as families have led them to deny any ability to feel. They both echo one another in their family structure: both are single child families, both depict relationships between parents and children as being remote, strained, even dysfunctional (although the view of the Burnhams is less extreme), in both cases it being the parents' attitudes which are responsible for the dysfunction (while the children show resilience). Individual (sexual) expression seems to be represented as the means towards forming the basis for secure values – not the family itself.

You might, therefore, ask how those representations shape our views of the family. The underlying view seems to be that the family unit is no longer seen as the root of social structures and values. Relationships, individuality and self-assertion take over that role. Families can't seem to avoid being oppressive.

However, the film concludes by suggesting that the importance of family values is precisely what is conventionally overlooked by people. Lester's restraint from sex with Angela suggests a shift from sexual desire to recognition of his paternal role and the values he has not appreciated: those of his family and his 'stupid little life'. And his final, momentary look at this 'stupid little life' shows that it's his wife and daughter which have meant most to him – without his having realised it.

Absence

In exploring how films might affect the way people see the world, it is just as important to recognise what is represented as well as what isn't. What is so conspicuous about this film – like popular TV shows like *Friends* – is the absence of any other ethnic grouping than white people. You might claim that the film intentionally focuses on the self-destructive nature of white, middle-class worlds, where race doesn't appear to impinge on this. And it is undoubtedly set in an area of the United States – commuter-belt Connecticut – which is white dominated. It should therefore remind audiences that the view of the United States conveyed in this film is restricted: it is not completely representative.

American Dream

As hinted at earlier, some of the key areas of representation – social groups, gender and race – hover around the way the film represents middle-class consumerism and what is frequently described as the American Dream. As several reviewers commented, there seem to have been a group of films which have recently challenged the materialism underlying the American Dream. I've already mentioned *Election*, *Happiness* or *The Virgin Suicides*. But as Phillip French pointed out in his *Observer* review, that sense of criticism in film dates back at the very least to the 1940s and earlier in literature (e.g., Scott Fitzgerald's *The Great Gatsby*, 1925, which has of course been filmed).

Happy Families?

What is the American Dream?

The broadest way of thinking about the American Dream is the belief that anybody, whatever their social background, can achieve success. The roots of that belief lay in the dreams of the early (white, European) settlers, who came to America in the early 1600s, hoping to create a new life for themselves. They dreamed of creating new communities, free from the religious persecution many of them were fleeing. Their dream was a simple, self-sufficient life, with communal rather than individual values at its centre.

Something of this ideal is suggested by the way the Amish community is represented in Peter Weir's 1985 film, *Witness*. The values represented there are of a society where communal values rather than individual ones are emphasised but also where materialism is denied at the expense of spiritual values. (You might notice, however, that the Amish are portrayed as a patriarchal culture.)

The dream of a self-sufficient life soon began to be equated with money and material success and focused on an exploited working class, who grew with the industrialisation of 19th century America and who understandably dreamt of material success. Their (American) dream was of an escape from their impoverished and exploited background to achieve the wealth and social status of the middle and upper classes, who benefited from their industrial labour.

Compare the way the family is represented in **American Beauty** *with* **The Virgin Suicides, Happiness** *and* **The Ice Storm.**

The climactic image of each film is a chilling comment on family dysfunction: the suicides in **The Virgin Suicides***; the electrocution image of* **The Ice Storm***; and the surreal representation of bourgeois family normality which closes* **Happiness.**

The disturbingly edgy representation of family normality in *Happiness*

4. Representations and the real

As Erin Brockovich's character shows, success is mainly achieved through individualism – a combination of perseverance, self-belief, assertion and ambition. In the more critical representation of the American Dream in American Beauty, *it is notable that the characters aspiring to material wealth are portrayed as salespeople – the classic embodiment of superficial people creating a superficial wealth and success. Some of you may know Arthur Miller's play,* Death of a Salesman *(1949), which depicts a salesman who gradually comes to realise that everything he has been striving for is worthless...ideas which strongly resonate in* American Beauty.

Dreaming...the American Dream: filmic representations

An interesting contemporary representation of that American Dream is Steven Soderbergh's *Erin Brockovich* (2000) and it provides a sharp contrast with American Beauty. The American Dream is represented positively in *Erin Brockovich*, as clearly something to strive for, whereas it is criticised and challenged in *American Beauty*. There is a confidence in everything the American Dream makes possible in *Erin Brockovich*. Erin, from a poorer background, achieves material success and status through assertion and determination after considerable perseverance. However, everything Erin aspires to – material wealth and status – is criticised and exposed to be empty in *American Beauty*. There seems to be no confidence in what the American Dream has to offer. The suggestion is that it is a way of thinking – an ideology – which deludes people. They strive for values which will turn out to be empty.

A revealing way of exploring that is to look at the scene where Carolyn interrupts Lester's love-making for fear of beer being spilt on the $4000 Italian sofa.

Gender and materialism

This film represents gender as being inextricably linked with materialism and the American Dream. For women – reflecting their ascribed roles – are represented as responsible for furnishing homes in an immaculate, but emotionally empty way and, indeed, to have matching pruning shears and gardening clogs. What they create is superficial – a mere image, like the artificially beautiful rose, the 'American Beauty' which Carolyn tends. Equally, being a man seems to involve being wedded to objects and lifestyles (related to consumer technologies – digicams, CDs, designer drugs, or red 1970 Pontiac Firebirds). The film suggests that self-expression ought to be defined in opposition to middle-class, materialist conformity and to gender stereotypes – but it isn't.

Ideological representation, ideological challenge...

American Beauty has attitudes – ideologies which are conveyed through its representations. And all the representations converge on ideological challenge: they challenge what I think is still a dominant ideology in America – that material success is important and is something everybody can achieve, irrespective of background, through hard work. *American Beauty* questions the values based on those aspirations.

To expose the ideologies – the values, attitudes and beliefs – underlying this film highlights the fact that the film-makers are providing audiences with more than a simple portrait of American middle-class society today. They are providing us with their version of society – a 'reality' which is actually a representation with points of view about what's being represented. By points of view, I mean that film-makers are conveying their attitudes and communicating what they think is important (their values) and what they believe in (their beliefs). That's what an ideological representation is. This takes us back to where we started in this section: that what is presented to us as 'reality' in this film is in fact an ideological representation which is constructed to look real. How is that done?

NOTES:

Conveying a sense of the real: realism

Realism is a way of conveying a sense of the real and in film terms can be achieved in several different ways.

Think about this simple distinction. A television soap opera like *EastEnders* aims to use sets, camerawork, editing, characters and storylines to convince us that what we are looking at is real. In other words it uses a set of **conventions** (ways of constructing sets, characters and storylines and ways of using cameras and editing techniques) to convey a sense of reality to audiences. *Hollyoaks* looks completely different, with its fast pace of editing, its frequent handheld camerawork and often distinctive lighting. But it is also aiming to convince us that what we're looking at it real. They both convey a sense of the real but in different ways, using the conventions of realism in different ways.

The conventions of realism

In essence, the conventions of realism are established ways of using the following main ingredients of films in ways which convince audiences that what they are looking at is real:

- *mise-en-scène* (including lighting & costume);

- camerawork;

- editing;

- characters;

- narratives;

- icons – symbols which immediately convince you of;

- sound.

The way those conventions are used have in fact been developed over a long period of time. In film terms, those main conventions were effectively established in Hollywood during the major studio era (between 1930 and 1948), although they drew on the experience of early cinema and the conventions have been modified slightly as technology has changed. Think of two popular films from that time like Michael Curtiz's *Casablanca* (1942) or John Ford's *The Grapes of Wrath* (1940). Both films use:

- studio sets and (studio-owned) locations to create a representation of Casablanca and California in the 1940s;

- lighting in a way which seems unobtrusive and natural;

- costume which is appropriate for people visiting a bar in Casablanca or being penniless in vagrant camps;

- a series of camera shots we now take for granted – establishing shots to establish locations, a standard variety of long shots and medium shots to film action interspersed with close-ups to show emotion;

- camera movement which follows action (tracking shots);

- camera angles to provide visual variety, create tension, give a sense of point of view and provide audiences;

- editing techniques like cutting to get from one scene to another, crosscutting between one scene and another to create suspense, filming from the same side of the action to give the impression of the audience observing action from one position (the so-called 180° rule, one element of 'continuity' editing, designed to create an uninterrupted visual flow of images for audiences);

- characters audiences can relate to and narratives which seem plausible;

- icons like the dress of the 'Okies' – synonymous with working people in the 1930s (*Grapes of Wrath*) – or German officer uniforms synonymous with the war and potential danger (*Casablanca*);

- sound which appears as part of the film's narrative – music in the bar at *Casablanca* (diegetic sound), the noise of empty cans in the settlement camp in *Grapes of Wrath* – and music to heighten the emotional atmosphere (tragic music in *Grapes of Wrath*, melodramatic music in *Casablanca*, non-diegetic sound).

These conventions are often called 'classic Hollywood realism' as they were conventions established in Hollywood and still used today, even if in an updated form to take account of changes in technology. If you compare a contemporary Hollywood film with one of these classic films from the past you will see the same conventions being used; but there will also be some slight variations. This itself suggests that the

Feelings replaced by objects...

Lester

'This isn't life. This is just stuff. And it's become more important to you than living. Well, honey, that's just nuts.'

Explore how cinematic features underline that criticism of Carolyn, materialism and the American Dream:

- *mise-en-scène*

- *depth of focus*

- *camera angles*

- *POV shots*

- *length of shots*

- *audience positioning*

4. Representations and the real

Dominant Ideology:

- the values, attitudes and beliefs that the majority of people hold.

- the way the majority of people see things in a society.

*Most people think that families are important. That's a **dominant ideology**. A film which supports that through the way it portrays families **reinforces** the dominant ideology.*

ET's (1982) representation of the family, like the majority of Spielberg films, reinforces dominant ideologies about the family.

*A film which questions whether families are more important than individuals **challenges** the dominant ideology.*

***Does** American Beauty **reinforce** or **challenge** dominant ideologies about the family?*

conventions of realism can change but that we accept both as attempting to convey a sense of the real to audiences.

More dramatic changes

The introduction of light-weight, portable cameras in the late 1950s gave rise to handheld camerawork, which was used particularly in more experimental art-house films of the day – notably French films of the late 1950s and early 1960s, part of the 'French New Wave', like Godard's *Breathless* (*A Bout De Souffle*, 1959) or *Bande A Part* (1964, which so influenced Quentin Tarantino). That kind of camerawork, influenced in fact by a documentary style of camerawork called cinéma verité, was the forerunner of the handheld camerawork used in the 1990s, most obviously by directors like Lars von Trier in *Breaking the Waves* or *The Idiots*. Like the *Hollyoaks* example earlier, this is a dramatically different way of using the conventions of realism – notably in camerawork and editing – but it is still a way of conveying the sense of the real. You could say therefore that there is not one single way of conveying reality but several, depending on how the conventions of realism are being used.

Take a short extract from the following films and ask:

- whether they are aiming to convey a sense of the real;

- how they use the conventions of realism to convey that.

Spike Lee, *Do the Right Thing* (1989);
Lars von Trier, *Breaking the Waves* (1996);
The Wachowski Brothers, *The Matrix* (1999);
Keith Gordon, *The Singing Detective* (2003);
Any Bollywood production you know.

What questions do they raise in your minds about realism?

The conclusions you may reach after exploring how the conventions of realism are used in contrasting films are that:

- there's not one realism but several 'realisms';

- no one form of realism is intrinsically more 'realistic' than another, even though they may attempt to convince audiences that this is the case;

- the conventions of realism vary from culture to culture;

- the conventions of realism vary over time and are constantly being extended and modified;

- audiences are constantly being presented with new devices which convince them that this is a new convention of realism (is the bullet time of *The Matrix* becoming a little like that?);

- realism is in fact an ideological representation of the real – the film-makers' version of reality.

Representation – Worksheet

Exploring the realism of American Beauty

American Beauty, with its three different 'looks', provides a fascinating way of exploring the conventions of realism. Each is subtly different from the standard conventions of realism.

Explore how the conventions of realism are used in:

Look 1 – the near Magritte take on American society

• Do editing and lighting and a tendency towards static camerawork, symmetrically composed framing give a more stylised look? What does that suggest about the 'realism' of those sections? Is the realism pointing towards challenge (realism with attitude)?

Look 2 – the fantasy sequences

• Is this a kind of psychological realism, a 'realistic' portrayal of fantasy, which itself relies on several conventions?

Look 3 – Ricky's digicam filming

• Is this 'more real' than Look 1, with obvious handheld sequences or just another version of reality (Ricky's)?

Realism and point of view: something to puzzle over

Sam Mendes, in his DVD discussion of the storyboards with Conrad Hall, has commented that this film is all about point of view. Is realism always about point of view – a version of reality with an implied point of view?

5. Production, distribution and exhibition

Nights in

Revenues from DVD/video sales now outstrip revenue from cinema screenings.

Finding Nemo – also incidentally with a soundtrack from Thomas Newman – rapidly became the first film where DVD sales exceeded US box office takings (which were very, very high).

Cinema screenings are almost becoming a further marketing tool for domestic sales in other formats.

Theatrical release: the release of films in cinemas.

Video/DVD sell through: the sales and rental of films in video & DVD formats.

Why study the film industry?

For most of us, watching films is a form of entertainment. Films are good for a night out or in and they probably make us think about aspects of our lives and the world we live in to some degree or other. What we tend to forget is that film is also part of an industry and, from the industry's point of view, is fundamentally a means of making profit. So, by the time you, as an audience member, pay your money to see a film, a lot of money has already passed hands. And (if the film's successful) a lot more money will pass hands in the future too.

You could therefore say that the film is seen differently depending on whether you're the industry or the audience:

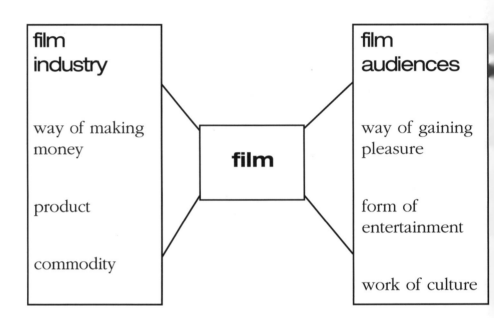

For the film industry, a film is a means of making money: it's a 'product' or a 'commodity' just like a can of baked beans or a mobile phone. The industry is obviously aware that the more appealing it can make its product to audiences, the more money it can make. And for audiences a film is a form of pleasure: it's an entertainment, a product of our culture and as such tells us things about ourselves and the world we live in. Indeed, films often do make us think about issues which they raise.

What we also forget is that there are many, many scripts which are never made into films; some which are made but not seen in cinemas; and others that are made but only seen in a few cinemas. So in a very basic sense, the industry dictates whether we see a film at all or whether it will end up in a cinema 'near us'.

NOTES:

But there's a further reason why the industry is important: for it is frequently responsible for shaping the film we see, or more subtly, building up expectations about the film we think we're going to see (through marketing). You are probably aware of famous cases where a film was changed in some way at a very late stage as a result of studio decisions (*Blade Runner* and *Fatal Attraction* (1987) are two classic examples).

What's the film industry?

The film industry is usually broken down into three phases, which represent the key stages from getting an idea off the ground to seeing the completed film in the cinema and on DVD or other formats:

Production

- securing finance for a film to be made;

- making the film – the production itself;

- covers everything, therefore, from the initial idea for the film, producing the script to the film's production and post-production (editing).

Distribution

- making copies (prints) of the film in order for them to be 'distributed' to cinemas across a particular country (cost of approximately £1000 per print);

- marketing (actively advertising a film, which costs money) and promoting the film (which doesn't);

- decides on where film will be shown – the 'release strategy'.

Exhibition

- showing a film at a cinema, on video, dvd or other formats.

Generally speaking there are different companies responsible for each of those phases – although increasingly, the same organisations either own or control all phases of that process.

> DREAMWORKS PICTURES
> presents
>
> A JINKS/COHEN COMPANY
> Production
>
> **AMERICAN BEAUTY**

American Beauty

These are the headline credits, taken from United International Pictures' Publicity Pack, who were the distributors of *American Beauty* in the UK. United International Pictures is the international distribution 'arm' of Universal and Paramount.

What do these credits actually mean? In simple terms, DreamWorks gave the producers, Jinks & Cohen, $15 million for the production in exchange for distribution rights. DreamWorks were effectively the main distributors and were responsible for the distribution of *American Beauty* in North America (actually carried out under franchise by Universal, with whom DreamWorks have a special distribution deal). They sold the distribution rights in the United Kingdom and Europe to United International Pictures (UIP). So when the credits say that a company 'presents' a particular film, it usually means they are the distributors.

The exhibitors of a film are the companies who own cinema chains and who can therefore show films. Cinemas in the United Kingdom are either part of the mainstream cinema chains – like Odeon, UGC, UCI, Warner Village or Showcase – or they are independent, so-called art-house cinemas. Many of those are also part of small chains: PictureHouse cinemas, for example, owns a chain of art-house cinemas in places like Brighton, Southampton, London, East Grinstead and Cambridge. *American Beauty* was shown at mainstream cinemas but how it reached those mainstream cinemas reveals a number of things about how films are released and exhibited. We'll follow the whole story of *American Beauty*, from its beginnings as a scriptwriter's idea to its final exhibition on screen, video and DVD. As with a number of things about *American Beauty*, what actually happened wasn't completely conventional.

Ever heard of these?

**Bodysong
Conspiracy of Silence
Silent Cry**

These were films made but never (so far) released theatrically.

Danny De Vito's Death to Smoochy *(2002) and* The Man from Elysian Fields *(2001), with Andy Garcia on the other hand were seen in the US but not the UK although they have now been released on DVD. This fate also befell Steven Soderbergh with* Full Frontal *(2002), despite his three previous films –* Erin Brockovich *(2000),* Traffic *(2000) and* Ocean's Eleven *(2001) – all being enormously successful.*

American Beauty

*Production Cost: $15m
US gross (first 9 months): $130m
UK gross (first 5 months): £21m*

In addition, the film will have earned more through theatrical release in other global markets and through DVD/video sell-through.

You can trace the exhibition of films by looking at imdb.com, a website actually owned by amazon.com.

---

5. Production, distribution and exhibition

'Steven Spielberg won't like this script. He'll hate it.'
- Alan Ball

'I had heard Steven talk on several occasions of his desire to make smaller movies, to make darker movies, to make the last movie you'd expect him to make.' - Bruce Cohen

Other DreamWorks productions of the time:
The Haunting *(1999)*
Forces of Nature *(1999)*
Gladiator *(2000)*
Almost Famous *(2000)*

'When it came to putting a director on the movie, the person we met and fell in love with was Sam Mendes.'
- Dan Jinks

Another reel story: from script to screen – the production phase

The writer Alan Ball, originally a playwright, had thought of the idea for *American Beauty* some eight or nine years before he actually wrote it. Immediately prior to writing the script, Ball had been scripting and producing the situation comedy *Cybill* and so was an established TV sitcom writer. Before he wrote the script, he hired a film 'features' agent, Andrew Cannava, who, to Ball's surprise, encouraged him with the *American Beauty* idea.

Pitching to an agent

'I started pitching *American Beauty*, which is not easy... "Well, okay, first of all, there's this whole trial going on and you think you know what happened but it didn't and then this kid with a video camera, he's kind of Zen and Buddhist..."'

'I was expecting Cannava's eyes to glaze over [because] I've been in so many pitch meetings where if you can't say it in one sentence you fail...Ninety per cent of agents in this town would've said, "Write the Julia Roberts story".'

- from an interview with Alan Ball by Nicholas Kazan, quoted in *Written By*, a journal for screenwriters, March 2000

Other DreamWorks Productions

DreamWorks productions: *Gladiator* (above), released the year after *American Beauty*, capped a remarkable period for the fledgling studio. Both films were critical and commercial successes, winning the Academy Award for Best Picture in successive years (1999 and 2000). *Gladiator's* DVD release was also a huge success, being one of the films that drove the dramatic rise in popularity of the format on its Christmas 2000 release.

NOTES:

That initial encouragement from Ball's agent eventually led to the completion of the film in April 1999. The key moments were these:

Dream to DreamWorks...

the pitch

mid 97: Pitching idea to agent, Andrew Cannava.

the script

June 97: Writing script whilst working on *Cybill*.

Feb 98: Finished script.

the agent – getting the producers

Feb 98: Agent Andrew Cannava generates interest amongst producers in Hollywood.

end of Mar 98: Script sent to Dan Jinks and Bruce Cohen, just starting their own production company – interested in doing 'smart, character-driven stories'.

getting the distributors

Bruce Cohen had worked for Amblin', Spielberg's production company prior to establishing DreamWorks. They feel DreamWorks might be interested in financing the production in exchange for distribution rights.

'DreamWorks, at that point, didn't buy a lot of material...It didn't seem like a DreamWorks movie because it seemed very independent. Very edgy, very dark, maybe a little small as far as budgets. They like their big John Williams films...then we thought this script is so good DreamWorks would be afraid not to buy it.' (Bruce Cohen)

the green light

late Spring 98: $15m budget given to *American Beauty* by DreamWorks

'[DreamWorks] was the highest offer but...it was such a low-ball figure. This is about going to the place that's going to make this movie and make it right.'
Alan Ball

Ball co-producer

DreamWorks made Alan Ball a co-producer, which is a way of allowing the writer to maintain control over what goes in the film.

script changes

Changes made to script – suggested by Walter Parkes at DreamWorks but considered by Alan Ball to improve script: for example, Lester does not sleep with Angela (Ball hesitated a lot over this point initially but was convinced by Parkes).

'[In the first draft] I had him sleeping with [Angela], but it wasn't sex. It was about making love. It was about this intimate connection between these two people. There is a moment of intimacy and connection where the idea of what they thought they wanted drops and then masks are dropped...[By not sleeping with her, however] he becomes the parent to her that he can't be to his own daughter.' (Alan Ball in article from *Written By*, March 2000)

Ball also decided himself to take out a flashback scene of Fitts having sex with a soldier in Vietnam to create more dramatic impact when he tries to kiss Lester.

director and casting

Jinks and Cohen were responsible for securing a director and for the casting. Of the 20 or so directors apparently approached, it was Sam Mendes whom Jinks and Cohen felt would be right. His background in the theatre, his passion for the script and his collaborative approach were what attracted both them and Alan Ball. And it was this collaborative approach which was to be the hallmark of the whole production, one which allowed everybody considerable creative freedom without producer interference.

shooting

Filming began in December 1998.

Post-production

Mendes jettisons the courtroom framing structure and his idea for a more whimsical opening with Lester flying into his bedroom to end up prostrate on the bed (the overhead shot of Lester actually used in the film).

before...

(Cybill Shepherd in *Cybill*)

...and after *American Beauty*

(Michael C. Hall and Lauren Ambrose in *Six Feet Under*)

5. Production, distribution and exhibition

Raising audience awareness – the distribution phase

Following the production and post-production phases, the film's distributors take over. They are responsible for the following main elements of film distribution:

release strategy & film positioning

- decisions to be made about the release strategy (wide, narrow, 'platform')

- decisions to be made about what date the film will be released, based on which films are likely to be the most advantageous to compete with (film positioning)

promotion (some costs) and publicity (free)

- press functions ('junkets') and press packs, offering information on film, its production, the main characters, the main actors, key production personnel and publicity stills

- talker previews (screening of film to opinion leaders, sometimes with film-makers present)

- magazine & newspaper articles/press reviews

- stars made available for television appearances (chat shows, interviews) or for special audience viewings

marketing (which is normally the major element of the distribution budget)

- advertising through poster images (used most obviously for billboard, magazine & newspaper advertisements prior to the theatrical release and on video and DVD for the home cinema market, now frequently more profitable than the theatrical release)

- cinema advertising – theatrical trailers, teaser trailers

- television advertising – TV trailers, teaser trailers (based on theatrical release trailers)

- website

producing ('striking') the prints of the film

- decisions to be made about the number of prints to be made of a film (a cost of around £1,000 per print)

For mainstream films, marketing costs can be between 30% and 50% of the total budget. In the case of *American Beauty*, although the figure hasn't been released, the release strategy would have involved substantial marketing. It underlines the fact that the release strategy is a crucial element to the commercial success of a film.

Marketing image

I'll start by thinking about the marketing of the film. The distributor needs to establish the primary audience for the film and provide an image for the film, which will appeal to, and thus sell to, that market. The distributor needs, in other words, to establish what in business terms is called the 'unique selling point'. Clues to that unique selling point are revealed in the main advertising image, which is used for posters and print advertisements as well as the all-important DVD and video covers.

The key marketing image for *American Beauty* is the close-up of a naked girl's midriff, with her hand suggestively resting below her navel and on an equally suggestive single rose bud. It is a teasingly sexual pose and is an example of the film's tagline – looking closer. Of course, the film will invite the audience to look more closely than the obvious connotations of this image.

The unique selling point: sex?

How do you know this film is sold in terms of genre?

Although Hollywood still (apparently) thinks of primary audiences as being male and between 15 and 24, this image is immediately interesting as it arguably targets younger as well as (riskily) 'less young' men and may indeed equally appeal to (some) girls and women as an example of sexual expectation and desire. As with the film itself, the image seems more obviously appealing to men.

The dominant feature of the image is therefore sexuality – of a young, possibly sexually flirtatious, sexually seductive kind, which invites male attention. It's men who are being teased into 'looking closer'. Sexuality dominates over stars (although Kevin Spacey's and Annette Bening's names are reasonably prominent, as are the references to awards – 5 Oscars, 6 Baftas – and the review extract, 'the BEST film of the year' (*The Sun*, simple and unambiguous). The typography – sans serif for film title and star references, with the trademark weighting of the font for 'Beauty' – again combines a younger audience – the modernity and accessibility of typeface – with more sophisticated design features, targeting the slightly maturer market (restraint, space, symmetry of design).

The marketing suggests that the distributors are trying through one image to simultaneously reach two audiences – the younger and the older.

The theatrical trailers seem to work in a similar way, appealing to the younger 18–24 audience as well as to the slightly more mature audience. The sequences used give equal emphasis to those sections of the narrative which feature younger and older characters. It gives the impression that the film is as much about Angela and Jane's sexuality and the 'psycho' next door (the 'teen' world) as it is about the mid-life emotional and sexual emptiness of the two parents (the adult world). The DVD includes two theatrical trailers.

The shorter of the two theatrical trailers – conceived as a teaser trailer, although it's a little longer than the average — is more focused and uses graphics, with narrative extracts to illustrate, rather than a voiceover. The music is electronic and light in tone – not the Thomas Newman score from the film itself, hinting that the trailers were prepared prior to the final sound

mixing – and leads to an overall climax of the fantasy rose images with a gun shot. There is a hint of suspense created – in line with a teaser trailer – in that Carolyn is shown sporting a gun and the sequence ends with the gun shot and the startled expression of Angela. Intertitles are used to punctuate the trailer and raise expectations of what the film's about – work, family, neighbours – only to suggest that you 'look closer' at the end of the trailer. Generic expectations are played with by visually juxtaposing 'If you think a comedy can't move you' with Ricky's 'Sometimes I think there's so much beauty in the world, I just can't take it'. Similarly 'If you think a drama can't be funny' is pitched against the 'You're so busted' moment at Mr Smiley's.

The full theatrical release trailer emphasises the 'Look closer' tagline much more and supersedes the teaser trailer with a more lyrical attempt to look closer at a street and a man and conjure up the more mystical beauty that Ricky and Lester eventually uncover.

In terms of dual audiences, it would appear that the teaser trailer appeals more to a younger audience and the full theatrical release trailer attempts to draw in both.

Marketing and different audiences – the website & television spots

The website demonstrates marketing which is overtly targeted at a younger audience. Look up the website – www.americanbeauty.com. You should see how its design and architecture targets younger viewers more.

Entertainment Weekly, in an article on Wes Bentley, pointed out how DreamWorks used the younger stars as a selling point:

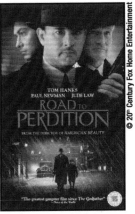

5. Production, distribution and exhibition

Joel Finler Archive

Targetting the teen market?

'Nighttime-tv dramas got promos touting top-billed stars Kevin Spacey and Annette Bening. Meanwhile, youth-oriented shows ran ads spotlighting Bentley, along with his young co-stars Thora Birch and Mena Suvari.'

Equally, UIP, who distributed the film in Britain, organised 'talker' previews for student audiences as one of their ways of targeting younger viewers. And in America, Kevin Spacey gave promotional interviews to student audiences after screenings across the country.

Perhaps the most significant element, however, of the distribution was DreamWorks' platform release, which had a large impact on the commercial success of the film.

Platform Release

The idea of a platform release – that is, to start showing a film with a small 'platform' of venues before increasing the number – is to generate as much positive word-of-mouth from reviews based on screenings in a restricted number of carefully selected locations. It was successful with films like *The Blair Witch Project* (1999) and *The Full Monty* (1997) and *Schindler's List* (1993) but failed with *Amistad* (1997), *Without Limits* (1998) and *LA Confidential* (1997). The film premiered at the Toronto Film Festival and immediately attracted its Audience Prize, together with the publicity which a major commercial festival like Toronto gives rise to.

The release pattern after its festival opening looked like this in America:

US Box Office

Week	Date	Number/screens	Box office ($k)
Opening w/end	19 Sept 99	16	861
2	26 Sept	429	5,939
3	3 Oct	706	8,188
4	10 Oct	1,350	9,505
5	17 Oct	1,459	6,608
6	24 Oct	1,528	5,180
7	31 Oct	1,553	3,324
Cumulative (9 months)			130,058

- source: imdb.com

What does this tell you about the release of the film in the USA? How does it compare with the UK (opposite)?

5. Production, distribution and exhibition

According to Jim Tharp, the head of distribution at DreamWorks, the company had a definite release pattern which was changed immediately to capitalise on its success in particular urban locations. The first change was to increase the number of screens on which the film was shown in the second week. And in some selected urban locations, advanced screenings were booked and Kevin Spacey made promotional stops. With this kind of platform release, the distributor has to support the film week by week with marketing and promotion but the commercial gains are substantial when it works. As Tom Sherak from 20th Century Fox put it the 'only one type of film that should be platformed [is] one that you believe in commercially.' The success of this platform release was arguably also due to a lack of fierce opposition in the US. Its release in the United Kingdom, handled by United International Pictures, was

scheduled for January and was carefully positioned amongst *Sleepy Hollow, Angela's Ashes, Stigmata, The Bone Collector* and *The World is Not Enough* (all 1999), all of which had been released earlier. *American Beauty's* main competition came from *Double Jeopardy*, which was released on 361 screens. (Information on platform release in Leonard Klady, 'The "Beauty" of platform success', *Variety*, 4–10 Oct 99.)

The success of the platform release was mimicked in the United Kingdom by generating considerable favourable publicity after the first week. Something like 75% of the available cinema sites (311) were used from the second week onwards. In the UK, only major (and probably genre film) blockbusters like *The Matrix Revolutions* would be shown on the very wide release, near-saturation totals of 400 plus screens from the beginning.

Week	Date	Number/screens	Box office ($k)
Opening w/end	30 Jan 00	23	425
2	6 Feb	311	2,386
3	13 Feb	310	1,654
4	20 Feb	311	1,523
5	27 Feb	311	1,178
6	5 Mar	302	863
7	12 Mar	319	713
Cumulative (5 months)			21,261

- source: imdb.com

What do you learn about *American Beauty*'s UK release from this?

Talker preview: where film is shown to opinion leaders in the hope of stimulating positive word-of-mouth views. The Full Monty (distributed by Fox Searchlight) was for example shown to women, hairdressers & taxi drivers!

Sam Mendes led some preview screenings in America, where response was very positive – which supported the idea for a platform release.

raining, hard. We can barely make out a row of TENTS through the downpour. We MOVE toward one TENT...

INT. TENT — CONTINUOUS (BLACK & WHITE)

CLOSE on man's hands gripping the wrists of another man. PULLING BACK, we see the YOUNG COLONEL'S face positioned over another SOLDIER'S — the Soldier from the photo — looking down at him as he pins him to the ground. Their expressions are intense, combative, deadly...then the other Soldier smiles and leans up to kiss the Young Colonel on the lips. As we continue to PULL BACK, we see they are both naked, and the Soldier's legs are wrapped around the Young Colonel's back. They fuck silently, their eyes locked on each other, until...

A blast of MACHINE GUNFIRE stops them abruptly. As they scramble to pull on their clothes, we HEAR the YELLS of other soldiers in the camp. The GUNFIRE increases in volume...

– Extracts reproduced in Nicholas Kazan, 'True Beauty', Written By, March 2000

What difference has the cutting of this scene made to the narrative?

5. Production, distribution and exhibition

Exhibition

Exhibition is the culmination of the film's cycle: it is how we all see the film, whether that is in the cinema or via DVD/video rental or purchase. Exhibitors gain their money from renting a film from the distributor but as has already been suggested, cinema exhibitors have very little control over the process. Mainstream cinemas have their programme dictated by weekly sales and by their head offices; and they in turn are reliant on the distributor, who is also checking which locations are better to show a particular film at. In America, for instance, *American Beauty* did less well in the more conservative South and rural MidWest, whilst it was in cities where the film flourished. In that case, the distributor decided on which locations would be able to keep the film and which had the film replaced. Similarly, local cinemas don't have a much of a budget for advertising. Local press adverts are the main source of advertising; on all other aspects of marketing, local exhibitors are reliant on the distributors to 'support' the film at particular locations through billboard and bus shelter poster campaigns and magazine and newspaper publicity.

The growing market is the DVD/video sell-through. DVDs have already exceeded VHS videos, which is looking as if it will be replaced. The major breakthrough has been that it appears that consumers are prepared to pay a premium for the 'extras' which are now a necessity for all DVDs. Hence, *American Beauty* includes what is now an increasingly common audio commentary, where the director and scriptwriter talk through the film shot by shot. (Sam Mendes' and Alan Ball's commentary is extremely revealing and informative.) It also includes a comparable discussion of storyboarded sequences with the cinematographer, Conrad Hall, as well as a featurette and two theatrical release trailers. The DVD is fast becoming the most significant format commercially.

Or to put it another way, the majority of profits from theatrical release will come from films, like *American Beauty*, whose budget is minimal compared to its eventual profits. For the majority, DVDs will continue to be the most significant format to generate profits. As already mentioned, the cinematic versions of films are almost becoming marketing vehicles for DVDs.

The recent multi-platform 'event', *The Matrix Revolutions*, demonstrates where celluloid films are heading. *The Matrix Revolutions* was screened theatrically in 109 locations around the world simultaneously. Previous films in the trilogy are showing in IMAX cinemas, have been released on DVD and video as well as in a computer game format. In addition, various spinoff narratives have been produced as the *Animatrix*. Industry figures are already speculating that cinema screenings may move away from celluloid to some kind of digital projection (potentially even broadcast by satellite) in the future.

Afterlife of film

The success of the film created its own afterlife. The Thomas Newman score was sampled for dance mixes and has appeared in advertising (most recently a jewellery advert, targeting men) and is selected by music editors for television programmes (recently used by BBC1's *Watchdog* for a report on suburban housing). And the fantasy image of Mena Suvari framed in rose petals was jokingly parodied for a *Radio Times* Wimbledon cover in the summer of 2000 – with Sue Barker's blonde head surrounded by strawberries.

Film images sell –
Sue Barker as stand-in
for Mena Suvari?

Production, distribution and exhibition – Worksheet 1

Nights out: 'sites and screens' you can visit

- How many cinemas are in your area?
- How many are independent (art house) cinemas?
- Does the table below suggest you are more likely to see mainstream, Hollywood films when you go out? Why?
- Do we all see the films *we* want to see of the ones the *film distributors* want us to see?

UK Cinema Circuits 2000

Mainstream			Company	Sites	Screens	Independent Cinemas (including film societies)	
Company	Sites	Screens				Sites	Screens
UGC	41	386	UCI	38	345	366	659
CineUK	20	219	Warner Village	33	331		
Odeon	118	634	Small Chains	54	159		
Showcase	19	244					

Total Screens: 2318 (Mainstream) 659 (Independent)

- Bfi Handbook, 2002

There are approximately 4 times as many places where you can see mainstream, Hollywood films – more if you take out all the private film societies.

Nights in: the rise of VHS and DVD

What does this rise of VHS and DVD tell you about film distribution?

1979	VCR population 230,000 (five years after VCR launched)
1980	Hollywood studios begin to enter rental market
1983	MGM/UA sold 20,000 VHS copies of *Poltergeist*
1984	First Disney animated Classic released: *Alice in Wonderland*
1985	First retail videos – 50 titles released in Woolworth's – sold a million copies in 6 months
1989	*Rainman* became the first 'straight to sell-through' film (not released in rental first)
1990	*Dirty Dancing* – first video to sell 1 million copies
1991	*Fantasia* – first video to sell 2 million copies
1993	Value of video market exceeded £1 billion *Jungle Book* – first video to sell 4 million copies
1997	*Star Wars* Trilogy box sets – worth £40 million
2000	*Gladiator* – first DVD to sell more than 100,000 copies in one week
2003	*Finding Nemo* – first film where North American DVD sales outperform total North American cinema box office (of $339m) in one week

- BVA Yearbook, 2001

Top 10 Films at UK Box Office 2000

1 **Toy Story**
2 **Gladiator**
3 **Chicken Run**
4 **American Beauty**
5 **Stuart Little**
6 **Mission Impossible II**
7 **Billy Elliot**
8 **X-Men**
9 **The Beach**
10 **Dinosaur**

[16 Erin Brockovich – Lucky for Alan Ball that he didn't write 'the Julia Roberts script'. See Alan Ball's pitching]

Top 10 Rental Videos in UK 2000

1 **The Sixth Sense**
2 **Gladiator**
3 **The Green Mile**
4 **East is East**
5 **The Deep Blue Sea**
6 **American Pie**
7 **American Beauty**
8 **Fight Club**
9 **The Mummy**
10 **End of Days**

Mena Suvari appeared in both **American Pie** *and* **American Beauty** *– were teen audiences drawn from one to the other?*

- *Pearl Harbour*, which disappointed at the box office, has so far made $326m from DVD sales and rentals.

- What else does this history tell you about the 'home cinema' market?

Production, distribution and exhibition – Worksheet 2

A few industry basics past & present

Big 5 and little 3 from Hollywood in the studio era, 1930–48 become what you could call the 'Massive 8':

1: Sony/Columbia

2: News Corp/20th Century Fox

3: AOL Time Warner

4: Disney, Buena Vista, Miramax

5: Paramount

6: Universal

7: DreamWorks SKG

8: MGM/UArtists

Research: who owns what

Find out:

(a) what else do each of the 'massive 8' own?

(b) how the following are relevant to the 'massive 8':

- horizontal & vertical integration

- synergy

- global media conglomerates.

Exploring marketing images (DVD/video covers)

Questions to ask

How is the film being sold? What are the dominant features of the image?

- Stars, genre, sexuality, director, awards, reviews?

What are the connotations of the image?

- Frequently gives clues to the distributors' sense of the target audience and helps show how that audience is being appealed to.

How is a particular audience being targeted (appealed to)?

- Image, tagline, typography, source of review?

Exploring trailers

Analyse the two *American Beauty* trailers using the notes below.

- Who is the target audience and how are they targetted?

- What visual images/sequences from the film narrative are chosen? How is the trailer edited?

- Does the trailer stress stars, genre, sexuality, action, dramatic tension?

- What music/sound is used and what are the connotations?

- Is a voiceover used? If so, what kind?

- What image are the distributors giving to the film?

Production, distribution and exhibition – Worksheet 3

Developing your screenwriting skills

Approaching screenplays – scripting one or two scenes (an AS Level task)

Aim to:

- develop an idea for a complete film and express it succinctly (around 200 words)
- think of the film in three parts – the 'three act' structure of Hollywood scripts
- visualise scenes – which will help realise what dialogue is required (think like cinematographers – even the director discussing what s/he wants with the cinematographer)
- script the opening of the film – might be a dramatic opening scene followed by a scene which establishes character and location (which is the case in *American Beauty*)
- express character and action in visual terms – which means using as few words as possible

Approaching screenplays – taking the skills further: scripting a group of scenes (more an A2 task)

Aim to:

- develop character(s) using minimum words
- develop your ability to visualise action
- think in terms of each scene including one key moment, either 'action' or a significant revelation a character
- construct dialogue *either* to lead up to that *or* start with it
- develop two related storylines which you can juxtapose to develop a more sophisticated sense of action

Production, distribution and exhibition – Worksheet 4

Writing a synopsis: working with American Beauty

Look at this synopsis, slightly adapted from *Sight and Sound*:

CONNECTICUT, THE PRESENT. Lester Burnham's life is cracking up: his wife Carolyn, an estate agent, and his daughter Jane both despise him; his new boss is threatening to fire him. Lester becomes obsessed with his daughter's schoolfriend, the sexually precocious Angela, after seeing her perform a cheerleading routine. Meanwhile, Ricky – the son of the Burnhams' new neighbour, a right-wing retired marine colonel named Frank Fitts – makes videos of Jane.

Pursuing his lost youth, Lester quits work and takes a job in a fast-food restaurant. He also starts to work out and takes recreational drugs supplied by Ricky. Carolyn begins an affair with her commercial rival Buddy Kane, and Jane and Ricky begin to fall in love. Lester finds out about Carolyn's affair when she and Buddy drive by his new workplace for burgers. Buddy breaks off the affair.

One night, Frank spies on Ricky and Lester. Because of the angle from which he sees them rolling a joint, Frank mistakenly concludes that Lester is paying his son to fellate him. Frank beats up his son, so Ricky prepares to leave home with Jane. Distraught, Carolyn drives through the night with a loaded gun. Frank confronts Lester but ends up making an advance, which Lester sensitively refuses. Lester finally gets a chance to have sex with Angela but on finding she's a virgin, grows paternal instead. Frank enters the house and shoots Lester. At the moment of his death, Lester sees his life pass before him and realises what a beautiful life it has been. (254 words)

Observations on synopsis:

The synopsis:
- includes reference to the location;
- places the key character at the centre of the story;
- introduces other characters;
- economically shows the relationship of the key characters;
- is structured in three acts, the 'beginning, middle and ending', corresponding to establishing character and action; the development, frequently, as here, following a dramatic change; the events leading to the conclusion. This is quite close to the idea of Equilibrium (Act 1), Disruption of equilibrium and its consequences (Act 2), Resolution of the action – events leading to the climactic closing action (Act 3). As we have commented earlier, *American Beauty* doesn't conform to a conventional 3 Act structure, but it does clearly involve three Acts;
- is a little longer than you might aim for.

Preparing further:

- Look up synopses of films in magazine reviews (*Empire, Total Film, Sight and Sound*, Film Guides like *Time Out* or *The Virgin Film Guide* or on the internet, e.g., imdb.com).
- Break them down into the three act structure, if they aren't written in that way.
- Look out to see whether they include the basic elements of a synopsis listed above.

Writing a synopsis for your own film - getting ideas

- Start with your own enthusiasms: think about three films you really like and why you like them. What is it about the narrative (i.e., screenplay) which really impressed you? This might help you identify ideas you can borrow – or effects you want to imitate.

- Think in terms of a genre which will provide a framework.

- Think about a major piece of action, within that genre, which involves at least two characters.

- Start to ask questions about the characters in your scene – flesh them out – see whether you can construct a story which culminates in that action.

- Decide on the structure of the way you will narrate the action: will it start dramatically with the action; is it told from a particular point of view; will there be any voiceover narration; how does it start – with some kind of teaser sequence (as with American Beauty) or a piece of dramatic action?

Production, distribution and exhibition – Worksheet 5

 Task

Writing a screenplay: working with American Beauty

The opening of films is always significant. What do you learn from the opening of *American Beauty*?

Scene 1 – Ricky: Do you want me to kill him? Jane: Would you?

- Dramatic opening – what makes it dramatic – in terms of script and visuals?
- What do Jane and Ricky say and why?
- What's the purpose of the scene?
- Note the way the scene incorporates an ambiguity.
- Note the way it's one shot, with the other character filming and off camera.

Scene 2 – Lester Burnham introducing himself and his family

- Establishing shot – what kind of establishing shot and why?
- Voiceover.
- Tone of voiceover.
- Starts with 42-year-old character, bored with his life, and surveys different elements
- Cameo shots of himself, his wife, their neighbours and his daughter – all visually and economically expressing key points about each of them – voiceover humorously punctuates what he feels/is like a point of view shot, reflecting his view of himself and his family.

 **Task**

'I've always wanted to kill her/him'- working on a screenplay opening

Rewrite *American Beauty*'s opening from a different point of view.

Base it on a 17 year old, bored with his family, talking about his parents – shift it from rich, middle-class neighbourhood to poorer area – Hughes Brothers' *Menace II Society* (1993) does that.

Have a dramatic event to start with – one of the parents' being shot but you don't know by whom? Your opening voiceover could begin or end with 'I've always wanted to kill her/him'.

How to set out your screenplay

The conventions for setting out screenplays do in fact vary. The key elements most commonly used are:

- Scene number.
- Interior/Exterior – Location – indication of time [BLOCK CAPITALS].
- Mise-en-scène (in italics), with reference to key SHOTS and CHARACTERS (Upper Case).
- Dialogue, preceded by character name, centred.
- Editing instruction – the transitions from one scene to another noted at end of scene (range right, Upper Case).

Example

12 INTERIOR: BRAD'S OFFICE – DAY

LOW ANGLE MEDIUM SHOT of Brad sitting behind his desk in his big office.

                    BRAD
I'm sure you can understand our need to cut corners round here.

                                        CUT TO:

HIGH ANGLE LONG SHOT of Lester sitting across from him, looking small and isolated.

                    LESTER
Oh, sure. Times are tight, and you gotta free up cash.

6. Spectators

Who are you? Would you describe yourself as a:

- **film spectator**
- **film viewer**
- **film consumer**
- **student of film**
- **reader of film**
- **film critic**
- **film fan**
- **film buff**
- **video/dvd junky**
- **internet pirate**

What do these different descriptions suggest about how people watch a film?

Do they mean that film viewers watch films in different ways? If you're a film fan do you watch a film differently from a film student? Or does film viewing combine different elements of all of those? Does that mean we all watch films in a variety of ways all the time?

There are other questions we can ask about film viewing:

- Do we just watch films in a passive way – visual popcorn? – or do we get actively involved in the dramatic images of cinema? Is much of cinema about spectacle – spectacular images and effects shown on a big screen with dramatic sound?

- Do we all see the same film – do we, in other words, all interpret the film in the same way, or does that vary depending on whether you're black or white, female or male, American, Asian or European?

- Do we watch films guided by publicity, stars or the promise of special effects?

- Do we see a different film when we watch it for a second or third time, as many of us do?

- Do we remember certain bits of the film and create our own version of the film in our minds? (DVD technology perhaps contributes to this process as several of us play favourite bits – chapters – rather than the film in its entirety.)

What these all suggest is that there's a little more to film viewing than first meets the eye. I'd like to explore all of these elements in relation to *American Beauty*.

What do <u>they</u> think? What do <u>you</u> think?

Young, white American female	- understands the social significance of setting the film in a small town in Connecticut. - identifies with Jane's view of her dad as a potential 'mid-life crisis geek' rather than as a man trapped by middle-class conformity. - fancies Ricky and considers whether they'd be prepared to take the risk Jane does in wanting to escape.
Young, black British male	- sees no black characters in the film. - relates to a male character like Ricky and his life-style. - identifies with the different kinds of female sexuality represented by Jane and Angela.
Middle-class British father	- recognises the desires of Lester (although might not be prepared to act on them). - responds to domestic problems and the sense of alienation Lester experiences at home. - sees the middle-class world as different from British – sees it as distinctively American.
Working-class American mother	- sees family as under threat by a level of materialism she doesn't have but might aspire to. - admires the way Carolyn fights in her terms for some kind of independence. - sees her role as mother as thankless and misunderstood by partner and children alike.

More on film fans later in this section.

Different interpretations

I'll start with what we've already touched on in earlier sections. Think about these viewers of *American Beauty* from Britain and America:

- young, white American female;

- young, black British male;

- middle-class British father;

- working-class American mother.

Of course, these are just general descriptions of types of people, which might themselves tend to stereotype how we think of those people. However, it is a way of teasing out the sorts of things that different audiences might respond to.

What this suggests is that people's experiences of film – the way we each see film – does vary, depending on social and cultural background. It implies that:

- viewers tend to be *selective* in their attention to films;

- what they 'select' – what creates a particular impact on them, what they respond to, what they remember – depends on their backgrounds;

- in other words, viewers' experience of film – what they make of it – differs.

Other interpretations: the Kevin Spacey film fan...

You could look at other kinds of viewer as well: the Kevin Spacey film fan will probably put a lot of emphasis on Kevin Spacey's body, his signature, apparently featureless facial expression which accompanies heavily ironic dialogue, his combination of the open and vulnerable, his tendency to confound the audience with enigmatic roles. It doesn't of course mean that this is the only thing the film fan will see in the film but it does suggest that her/his experience of the film will feature Kevin Spacey.

...the film student...

Equally the film critic or film student might be responding to the cinematographic features of the film and the way they underline and contribute to the overall issues the film raises.

...gay people...

Gay people might well see the film as mainly about the way it indirectly raises the issue of people's responses to gay people and the consequences of sexual repression. Fitts' behaviour could indeed be thought of as a reflection of a large part of society's doubtless continuing disapproval of same-sex relationships and homosexual orientation.

Different film experiences, different conditions of viewing

Similarly, the circumstances in which we watch American Beauty can affect our experience of it. Again, think about the different kinds of experience viewers get from the following:

Watching in a mainstream cinema	• full impact of cinematography and lighting very apparent. • soundtrack striking.
Watching in cinema with friend/boyfriend, girlfriend or group of friends	• you're sometimes aware of person next to you and how they would react to a scene. • many people talk about the film afterwards – would a group of girls/group of boys talk about the film in the same way – are you affected by what others think about a film?
Watching the film on television with parents	• small screen. • visual impact not so dramatic as cinema. • some embarrassment about watching this film with parents. • tend to be particularly aware of moments involving parents, their sexuality, their potential inability to communicate with children.
Watching film on DVD (on your own?)	• watch extras. • audio commentary might lead you to seeing film in a different way. • do you think about the film differently because of what a director says? • do you play some sequences more than once?
Using internet (might even attempt to download film at some stage in future)	• finding out about different viewers' experiences of the film. • finding out what's been said about film. • responding to film publicity. • actively contribute to views/chat rooms. • your views about film become shaped by others' experiences of film.

6. Spectators

Why was this scene cut? What difference would its inclusion have made to the film?

The experiences viewers gain do seem to relate to three, perhaps obvious, sources of pleasure: *emotional* pleasure (response to image and sound, narrative and genre); *sensory* pleasure (the visual and aural impact of film, particularly emphasised in cinemas); and *cognitive* pleasure (the way we think about what we've seen and engage with ideas and issues in whatever form that might be). It's probably the case that those experiences are not easily separable but they do suggest that there are different elements which make up people's responses to films.

Same film, different experience

Everything suggested so far suggests that we don't all watch films in the same way; and I also think that the *circumstances* in which we see films affect the way we respond to them. We don't watch films in the same way because we all bring a different experience of, and awareness about, the world we live in to films: our social and cultural backgrounds vary. And the kinds of pleasure we derive from film similarly varies.

Films, therefore, can and do affect audiences in different ways: they come to mean different things to different audiences. It suggests that films don't therefore have a single meaning but several meanings and those meanings will reflect the different social and cultural backgrounds of its audiences. Formally this is described as *pluralism*.

Positioning: negotiated, oppositional and preferred interpretations

Having stressed the different ways different groups of people tend to look at films, it's interesting to observe how lots of people do nevertheless share points of view, experiences and interpretations about the film. This suggests that a film like *American Beauty* encourages viewers to think in a particular way (positions them to accept a 'preferred' interpretation). Equally it cannot legislate against some viewers taking an opposite point of view about the film but in reality the majority of us find ourselves developing a point of view based on a mixture of our individual social and cultural experiences and what the film encourages us to think.

This is highlighted by one of the more controversial aspects of *American Beauty*: Lester's desire to have sex with Angela. The film does effectively position us to identify with Lester and applaud him for refraining from sex and becoming suddenly paternal. The narrative, cinematography, acting, mise-en-scène, editing all encourage us to recognise what Lester comes to recognise: that he is a father and that what he most values is his family. Immediately after his attempt to sleep with Angela – represented as subtle and sensitive, masculine behaviour – he asks Angela about Jane. It is by seeing past Angela that he sees the real beauty in his 'stupid little' life – Carolyn and Jane.

However, some female viewers objected to the near sanctification of Lester and the corresponding demonisation of Carolyn. Their reading would clearly be an **oppositional** one. My own responses combine the two: both Lester and Carolyn – neither of whom are at face value attractive characters – are shown as trapped and it is through sexual desires that both of them achieve some faint sense of liberation. For Lester, it is literally short-lived, but is nevertheless something he recognises before his death; and for Caroline, all that she has recognised, is pitiably lost (expressed in that moment before the closet – is it Lester's clothes she's grasping?). You might say that what I am doing here is **negotiating** a response based on what the film suggests and my own experiences.

The interesting aspect of *American Beauty* is that so much of the film, in keeping with its subject matter, is controversial and develops preferred readings: attitudes towards sexual orientation and to Fitts in particular; attitudes towards recreational drugs; attitudes to sexual relations between younger and older – the painful sense in which there's a tension between what most would accept as morally wrong, between a recognition of the plausibility of Lester's position and Angela's. Lester's desires are based on questionable (but understandable?) male fantasies of younger girls; and Angela's desires are based on her fantasies about older men. They are both perhaps as exploitative and vulnerable as one another.

Spectators as voyeurs?

Related to the idea that films position viewers to adopt particular points of view and thus shape their views, is the idea of the voyeuristic, male gaze. Have a think about your film viewing for a minute. Would you agree that in most of the mainstream films you know:

- cameras linger more frequently on women and women's bodies than they do on men and men's bodies?

- women's bodies are more frequently shown in sexually suggestive poses than men?

- we see more naked women than naked men on screen?

Test this out by thinking of five films you've seen recently and ask whether they tend to do all of the above.

If you agree with these statements, you are agreeing with many of the claims Laura Mulvey made in 1975, and which have been debated constantly since. She argued that films tend to show events, and particularly women and sexuality, from a male point of view. Films therefore encourage viewers to see films from a male perspective, whether they are male or female. Viewers adopt what she called a 'male gaze'. If you are a woman you are encouraged to see yourself and your sexuality in terms of men and men's desires. You become an object of men's control. And all of this happens without you being aware of it as a result of camerawork, the way films are edited and film narratives themselves.

Whereas there are still plenty of films which tend to reflect a male perspective, it is also true to say that Hollywood and independent cinema have challenged the 'male gaze' to varying degrees. Hollywood in the 1980s has introduced strong, female leads into its action films, for example *Aliens* (1986), the *Indiana Jones* series (1981—1989) and *Terminator 2* (1991). In the 1990s, 'girl power' emerged, moving from Madonna (look at David Fincher's *Express Yourself* music video) to, more recently, Lara Croft in *Tomb Raider* (2001) and *Charlie's Angels* (2000). In these films women are shown to be more in control of their sexuality – sexual *subjects* rather than sexual *objects*, you might say – but it is debatable whether they still encourage a male gaze. Lara Croft's sexuality may show power and control but it still panders to male sexual fantasy and the male gaze. Alternatively, however, female audiences may respond differently and place more emphasis on control through sexuality.

As you might expect, independent films have challenged the male gaze and raised gender issues by attempting to build in different kinds of camerawork and editing to their narratives. Maggie Greenwald's *The Ballad of Little Jo* (1993), Jane Campion's *The Piano* (1993) and *The Portrait of a Lady* (1997). Allison Anders' *Gas, Food, Lodging* (1992) and *My Crazy Life* (Mi Vida Loca) (1993) and Kimberly Peirce's *Boys Don't Cry* (1999), all challenge women's role in society in several ways and attempt to portray sexuality from a woman's point of view. *The Piano* actively presents a naked Harvey Keitel for the camera's, and the female character's, gaze. Patricia Rozema's film *The White Room* (1990) effectively asks the question of whether film viewing is voyeuristic. Patricia Rozema parallels the voyeurism in the narrative with that of the film viewer, as in Hitchcock's *Rear Window* (1954) and Powell's *Peeping Tom* (1960). And Jane Campion's recent *In the Cut* (2003), like Kathryn Bigelow's *Blue Steel*

Sigourney Weaver as Ripley (and Carrie Henn as 'Newt') in *Aliens* (1986)

Linda Hamilton as Sarah Connor in *Terminator 2* (1991)

Angelina Jolie as Lara Croft, *Tomb Raider* (2001)

Girlpower: Role models for women or sex fantasies for men?

For more on male gaze, female and queer gaze, see Jill Nelmes 'Women and Film' in **Introduction to Film Studies**

6. Spectators

A more detailed look at the different kinds of gazes played with in The Piano is in Jill Nelmes' article, mentioned above, where there is a case study of The Piano.

(1990) before it, aims to raise these issues in a more mainstream context and portray sexuality from a female point of view.

Equally some independent films in the 1980s and 90s have shown a gay gaze – incorporating a camera style which overtly foregrounds gay sexual orientation. Derek Jarman's *Caravaggio* (1986) and Rose Troche's *Go Fish* (1994) are good examples

American Beauty and gendered camerawork

American Beauty is a good text for exploring the questions:

- is there such a thing as camera gaze, whether from a male, female or gay perspective?
- is camerawork always linked to a particular point of view, whatever that is?

Like *Rear Window* and *Peeping Tom* – metaphors for the link between voyeuristic camerawork and a possible male-oriented voyeurism of cinema spectators – *American Beauty* plays with the idea of a potentially voyeuristic camera (i.e. Ricky's digicam filming), only to reveal that all's not quite what it appears.

© Pathé Pictures

In the Cut aims to position audiences to see events from a female point of view. Does director Jane Campion succeed?

NOTES:

Conclusions

Finding a direct answer to the questions posed at the beginning of the section is very difficult with such a controversial topic. *American Beauty* itself seems to play with the idea of voyeurism, camera gaze playing against audience expectations so that they do eventually look closer. Everything I've suggested implies that audiences are being led to question what they see and challenge the idea of a male gaze. The most conspicuous comment in the film is where Jane grabs Ricky's camera and starts filming him. *American Beauty* actively challenges the idea of audiences' being male-oriented voyeurs and, as with the issue of realism, it seems to be suggesting that it's not possible to see camerawork outside the context of points of view.

Having said that, I nevertheless feel that mainstream films continue to encourage a male gaze but that the way female and male audiences respond to those images is not as stereotypical as it would first appear.

Fans' eye views: what's fandom about?

Having considered how camerawork affects audiences, I'd now like to turn to a specialised audience: fans. Fans are not obsessive geeks – although that's the most familiar image. Genre fans like Trekkies or horror fans (have a look at the great send up of sci-fi fans in *The Simpsons*) or idolising younger fans relishing every gesture of a Leonardo Di Caprio, George Clooney, Julia Roberts or Uma Thurman seem to give that impression. A lot of people who would describe themselves as fans are simply people with intense enthusiasms. What links all fans, however, is that they are:

- selective about what they like;
- they turn their enthusiasms into something personal and;
- they share those enthusiasms with other like-minded people.

The media and film writer, John Fiske, makes those points when he describes fans:

'...[they] select from a repertoire of mass-produced and mass-distributed entertainment certain performers, narratives or genres and take them into the culture of a self-selected fraction of the people. [What they select is] then reworked into an intensely signifying popular culture that is both similar to, yet significantly different from, the culture of more 'normal' popular audiences.'

The Cultural Economy of Fandom (1992)

As a result of 'reworking', for example, film stars into an 'intensely signifying' experience, fans see films differently. The way they view films is dominated by their specific knowledge and enthusiasms for that star. That suggests in turn that they may place less emphasis on what a film suggests – the messages and values, the ideologies raised by its narrative – and more on the significance of stars' performance and perhaps those elements of the narrative which relate to the star. It's claimed that fans of stars and actors, for example, view films like this:

- in relation to other films in which the fans' star or actor appears in (intertextuality);
- in terms of the star and the star character's point of view and;
- through their own (sexual) desires and fantasies for the star him or herself.

That suggests a very different way of making sense of a film. It places more emphasis on fans' emotional responses and on messages and values arising from the star's performance. It consequently challenges the view that one may have as a student of film – which is that it's the 'messages and values', the ideologies, of films which are the most important element in film viewing.

Studying fans' interests raises another issue. It raises the question of how far fans' enthusiasms are being shaped, even dictated, by the film industry and the media it attempts to influence through publicity and promotion. Are fans, in other words, just another exploitable commodity?

6. Spectators

Henry Jenkins in another classic article talks about the 'social nature of [fans'] interpretive and cultural activity.' Fans adopt a 'distinctive mode of reception, involving conscious selection and repeated consumption of material; and translation of the material, and its reception, into a social activity...' Fandom is a 'particular interpretive community'.

'Strangers no more we sing' in Lisa Lewis, 1992 – see Going Further

What do you think Henry Jenkins means by this?

Researching fans: There are a growing number of what are called 'ethnographic studies' to uncover audience reactions. A good start to (academic) writing on this are Melvyn Stokes' & Richard Maltby's two books: Identifying Hollywood's Audiences (1999) and Hollywood Spectatorship (2001).

www.thora.org

http://users.aol.com/macparrot/scrapbook.html

6. Spectators

Web communities

When you look on the web, you see unofficial as well as official fan sites; and you also see some companies which are creating sites for fans to exchange views. That underlines the question of whether fans become an exploitable commodity by the film industry. How far, in other words, are fan behaviour and fans' attitudes controlled by the film industry?

I suggest that fan behaviour and enthusiasms are shaped strongly by the industry, who set the agenda (i.e., provide the framework for discussion) for the majority of fans' enthusiasms and indeed the way they discuss issues which emerge about stars. The image of Kevin Spacey as a stage (and thus character) actor features in most articles about him and is firmly part of the way he's promoted. For example:

> 'For the last years he's been importing the serious dedication craft and material that characterises a good actor and bolting it to the more populist medium of the movies.' *Empire*, Feb 2000

> 'Spacey's career has been defined by his gift for slithering in and out of the audience's grasp on his characters...[he] has displayed a rare gift for inhabiting difficult parts.'
> *Observer Monthly*, Mar 2003

And the *American Beauty* press pack, confirming the industry's promotion of this image, devotes two paragraphs to his stage career, which included appearing opposite Liv Ullmann in an Ibsen play (*Ghosts*) and opposite Jack Lemmon in Eugene O'Neill's *Long Day's Journey into the Night*. This press pack is, of course, intended to assist journalists in writing their articles.

His stage acting is a frequent discussion point on websites – normally to guarantee Spacey's pedigree. So too, however, is his sexual orientation. Speculation that Spacey might be gay was popularised by the *Empire* article of February 2000, referred to above (Spacey featured on its cover, at the time of the UK release of *American Beauty*). Spacey refused to enter into the debate as if protesting his heterosexuality might indirectly be suggesting that there's something wrong in being gay. Interestingly, fans tend to deal with such claims by balancing them against his much publicised right to privacy and his commitment to character acting. You could therefore conclude that fans' attitudes are both directly and indirectly shaped by industry publicity.

NOTES:

Spectators – Worksheet 1

Ricky's gaze – exploring Ricky's obsessive digicam filming

Questions to ask:

- Do you think Ricky's camerawork is voyeuristic?
- Does the camerawork exploit women, turn them into the sexual object of his lens and assert his power over them?
- Does his camerawork encourage audiences to think in a stereotypical male way?
- Does it raise questions about gender? In what way?

1: Opening shot of the film, in Ricky's bedroom, extracted from the sequence played in context later –

- *Despite the concentration of the camera on her face, is Jane relaxed being filmed? Is this encouraging a male gaze?*

2: Filming her from darkened veranda, Jane challenges Ricky:

- Is the camerawork exploitative? What's the significance of the way Jane challenges Ricky and is then shown being flattered by his attention when she moves into the house?
- What's the significance of the scene the following day when he apologises and says that he's 'just interested' in her?

3: Filming Angela and Jane from his room:

- What's the significance of his camerawork zooming past the flirting Angela and fixing on Jane's smiling expression on the mirror?
- What's the significance, in a later scene, of Jane revealing her breasts to him at which point he, seemingly oblivious to this, zooms in for a close-up of her face?

4: Filming in Ricky's bedroom:

- In a quite natural way Jane challenges Ricky's male authority by grabbing hold of the camera and turning the camera on Ricky. What is being suggested by this scene?

Reflections

Sam Mendes says that Ricky is reaching out towards Jane with his camera. Is he deliberately playing with the idea of the male gaze and voyeuristic camerawork and suggesting that the camera here is part of a reciprocal relationship?

As Ricky's camera is a means of recording and observing what lies below the surface, is that inviting us as audiences to look beyond the superficial idea that it is voyeuristic?

Jane grabs the camera: a deliberate challenge to Ricky's camera control?

Spectators – Worksheet 2

More on gaze...
Lester's gaze – exploring how his fantasies are presented

Lester's fantasies are in an obvious way, male-oriented, as you would expect:

• Is it significant that they are very clearly shown as Lester's fantasies and from his point of view?

• Is the narrative context significant?

Just Lester's fantasy or *all* male viewers' fantasies?

   - that he holds back from having sex with Angela and comes to realise this would be wrong. It becomes the means for his realising what is important to him.

   - that Angela actively encourages the relationship.

Reflections

The film places emphasis on audiences' understanding the context of the camerawork. Does this suggest that camera gaze is less of an issue about how camerawork is used but more on how audiences interpret it?

Fitts' gaze

You might notice that the apparent voyeurism of Ricky becomes the real sexualised voyeurism of Fitts as he stumbles across the disk of Lester (having thrown out the one of his wife). You first of all think that Fitts is simply uncovering what he supposes are Ricky's voyeuristic shots of Lester and evidence of some kind of relationship. Only later do you come to recognise that the images were a voyeuristic act for Fitts.

Fitts as voyeur? A brief, chance encounter

Spectators – Worksheet 3

Researching on the web

A *site to start:* There are frequently revealing comments on the Internet Movie Data Base site. There are user comments on film entries and message boards for both films and actors: www.IMDb.com (owned by amazon.com)

Searching: The obvious place to start looking is with the Google search engine: www.google.com

You can distinguish between official and unofficial sites by addresses. Look for distributors' names in the address.

Kevin Spacey

You might look up:

- www.drivingmrspacey.com

- Sputnik Central! The Kevin Spacey page – users.aol.com/macparrot/kspacey.html (a site created by a fan, Jennie Parrot in the mid 90s. Includes a photo scrapbook.)

- A fan listing site – www25.brinkster.com/swankyfunk/kevinspacey.html

What do all the contrasting photographs of Kevin Spacey suggest about fans?

In 2003, Spacey set up and launched TriggerStreet.com, a site encouraging aspiring film-makers to submit screenplays for development. Trigger Street Productions is the name of his own production company. (Interestingly kevinspacey.com, his original site, became the subject of a cybersquatting case in 2001.)

Thora Birch

www.thora.org

Her official site is the conventional, glamorising one – attempting to create a glamorous image through graphics and photographs. Something of her screen image comes through 'The Fan Interview'.

Spectators – Worksheet 4

Fans' views

There are two obvious ways of exploring fans' views and both involve research. You can:

- ask yourself, friends (of all ages) and family about whether they are fans of a particular film star or actor or film genre;

- explore fans views through internet sites, where 'communities of interest' are being established.

How far do you agree that fans look at films in a different way from general audiences? In order to give focus to your research, you might explore how far you agree with John Fiske's claims made about fans' distinctive viewing experience.

> '...[they] **select from a repertoire of mass-produced and mass-distributed** entertainment **certain performers, narratives or genres** and take them into the culture of a self-selected fraction of the people. [What they select is] then **reworked into an intensely signifying popular culture** that is both similar to, yet significantly different from, the culture of more 'normal' popular audiences.'
>
> John Fiske, 1992

Interviewing fans of stars and actors

Start by interviewing yourself and then interview other people:

- Make a note of key phrases from your own and other's replies.

- Record the interview with a compact tape recorder or get more creative and video the interview.

Planning your own interview

'Selecting from mass-produced entertainment...'

- What is it about your chosen star that you like so much?

- How did you first get interested in your chosen star – a particular role, even some particular scenes or shots in specific films?

- Which of the roles your chosen star has taken is your favourite?

- Do you fancy your star? Is the star's sexuality, even in a fantasy-like way, part of what you like about your star?

'Making the experience more significant...'

- Do you talk about your star with friends or on the internet?

- Do others' views influence the way you see your star?

- Are there particular aspects of your star that have become very significant for you (and your friends)?

- Do you have a particular image of your star?

- Do you read magazines/watch interviews/DVD extras/use the internet to find out more about your star?

- What have you found out about her/him?

'Responding to the film in terms of the star, seeing the film in relation to other films the star has appeared in...'

- What for you were the most memorable moments in your favourite film featuring your star?

- Do they involve your star?

- Is your view of the film influenced by your star's appearance in it?

- When you're watching your star in a particular film, do you find yourself comparing that role with another one?

- Does your star play a character which is similar to his or her public image?

- Do you have a collection of videos and/or DVDs featuring your favourite star? Do you watch particular scenes in films?

Spectators – Worksheet 5

Following up on your research: analysing the results

Look through the interviews and see whether they conform to the points writers like John Fiske have claimed about fans. Do you think these fans watch Kevin Spacey or Thora Birch films in the same way as those of us who are not fans?

List your results in a table like this.

Selecting from mass entertainment industry	Relating stars to other films they appear in (intertextuality)	Making sense of the film in terms of the star	Reworking the star into something highly significant/seeing the star in terms of their sexuality

You might also note that several of the people interviewed thought about the star in ways similar to the image created by the industry. Kevin Spacey is, for example, frequently portrayed in magazine journalism and reviews as a serious character actor – as indeed he is; much is made of his privacy (at the same time as printing articles on him); and the issue of his sexual orientation often gives rise to comment. Does this have a bearing on the point made about fans, that their views are shaped indirectly by the film industry and its publicity and promotion? The same point is echoed by fans on the web.

Spectators – Worksheet 6

Spaced out on the enigmatic Spacey...

Here are the views of some fans of Kevin Spacey and Thora Birch who I interviewed.

22-year-old female

I really love his face – it's cool, blank, always on the edge of a smile. As if he's about to make a sarcastic comment. And I really love his voice. It's a bit like his face – I don't know, it seems not to have any particular features. I don't know what it is but his voice does turn me on. To me it's quite realistic that Angela fancies him in *American Beauty*. I've chatted about this on-line and several of us said the same. He's a bit of a puzzle, I suppose. You can't quite make him out – but that's somehow thrilling.

Female in her 30s

He's just such a great actor. His stand-up and theatre background are important. He's got charisma – he's got hidden depths. He really brings something to all the films he's in. I talk to one or two friends about him – there's a person I work with [male, similar age] who's a real fan of Spacey too. We both agree about his acting, which is what we really like about him.

...I really respect him that he keeps his life private, even to the point of not entering into the debate over his sexual orientation. That was all ridiculous anyway. All the films he's in are not the conventional, mainstream Hollywood films but have got something different about them. He chooses his roles...

American Beauty really blew me away...Spacey was brilliant in it.

Male 18

Spacey is such a great actor. *The Usual Suspects, LA Confidential, Shipping News* – I thought he was great in all those. I've got DVDs of the whole lot – at least everything I can get hold of. I love that scene in the kitchen in *LA Confidential*...and the opening of American Beauty with its voiceover is so funny...I liked the way he kind of blackmailed his boss when he walked out on his job and the scene where he's with Carolyn in the living room playing with the remote-control car. And when he busted Carolyn. And when he shares a joint with Ricky. I liked the funny bits. In fact, the whole rebellion thing was cool.

There's more to American Beauty, Thora Birch...

Male 17

You were kind of carried along by the film. This was the first film I saw her in. We all talked about it at the end of the film. We all fancied Mena Suvari like mad and spent a lot of time talking about whether we would or wouldn't have. If we were in Kevin Spacey's position. Or even if we weren't! Then somebody said would you just drop everything and walk out on your parents like Thora Birch? I think we probably created a Thora Birch fan club right there but we didn't know it.

I think Paul Thomas Anderson is a great director and I saw [Terry Zwigoff's] *Ghost World* because a friend said it's a bit similar. It's not really but Thora Birch was in that too. And she was amazing. She plays the same sort of really independent girl there. Just more weird. I've since become a real fan and I regularly check her site. If I knew more about websites, I'd probably create one. She's made to look more sexy on her site but her personality comes through in the interview....My favourite moment in *American Beauty* is that scene up against the white wall when she sort of smiles at Wes Bentley. A defining moment – more in it than you think.

Female 18

She was a really interesting character. I used to have a friend a little like Angela. Well, I still see her. It's easy to relate to. I've seen her in most of her films and what I like about her is the way she is able to play these independent girls who are really cool. Like Gareth, I thought *Ghost World* was a fascinating film. The glasses were funny. And the way she dresses. She played opposite another pretty girl in that film, who was a bit morestraight – Scarlett Johansson.

Interviews carried out by the author.
Many thanks to all who participated.

Questions

What do you learn about the way fans look at films from these interviews?

Do they support what John Fiske said about fans?

Auteur and genre films

Have a look again at the credits for *American Beauty*. There are around 18 credits for those the press pack calls the 'film-makers', a further 150 credits for the crew (another 36 for the second filming unit) and some 39 actors. Bearing in mind that over 200 people worked on this film, *American Beauty* is obviously not the work of one person. And yet we frequently refer to films as though they were. There's Steven Spielberg's *Saving Private Ryan* (1998), Martin Scorsese's *Goodfellas* (1990) or Jane Campion's *The Piano* (1993), for example. On the other hand, there are some films we'd find it hard to name the director. How many directors of Bond films can you list?

You could claim that films tend to be thought of either in terms of their director or their genre. If audiences think of a film mainly in terms of genre, you would describe it as 'collaborative'. In this case, the director is one of a team working on a well-established genre, where there's little room for individuality. If audiences think of a film as the product of one individual's 'vision', normally the director's, and bears their 'signature' so to speak, you would describe the film as an 'auteur' film, where the director is an 'auteur' (French for 'author'). That implies the director is like an author of his or her own work and has control over how the film will be made. This of course means that some directors are considered 'auteurs', fully in control of the way the film will eventually turn out, whilst others are thought of as simply following the scripts. You might claim that lots of 'made for television films' fall into that category. However, there are several films where there is a real tension between whether it is the genre or the director's contribution which is the more important. You might indeed list Spielberg here: are some of his films more 'auteur'-like than others? Does *Saving Private Ryan* suggest more of an individual guiding vision than the *Indiana Jones* trilogy? Or is *Raiders of the Lost Ark* (1981) a markedly different kind of action film and *Saving Private Ryan* too reliant on the conventions of a World War II film?

Auteurs

What defines an auteur is 'personal vision' rather than mere 'technical mastery', to use words of Lawrence S Friedman (*The Cinema of Martin Scorsese*, 1997). Or as Patrick Phillips puts it – 'an auteur director is one who brings to a film signs of their own originality'. From that point of view, directors are not the only 'auteurs' in film-making. Other figures crucial to making films can bring individuality to their work. A cinematographer, actor, screenwriter, studio or even a composer could be thought of as being an auteur. An 'auteur' implies that their work is individual and linked either stylistically or thematically (or both). Hence, writers on film frequently talk in terms of an auteur's signature or their distinctive features.

The real issue for audiences is how an auteur's contribution makes meanings for them – frequently through reference to other films the auteur has made. Auteurs consequently have sufficient control over the film-making process to be able to follow their 'vision' and incorporate their stylistic and thematic interests. An auteur's contribution creates additional significance for audiences, which audiences respond to by drawing on their knowledge of other films made by that auteur. It is thus an obvious example of how audiences respond 'intertextually' to films: additional meanings are created by references to other films.

Debates and backgrounds

The question over whether films should be thought of as a collaboration rather than the product of one single person's guiding vision, like a director's, has been a significant debate over the last 50 years or so – particularly within film studies itself. There are two main issues here:

- Do we tend to think that an 'auteur' film is more important than a collaborative genre film?

- Do we tend *only* to think of directors as auteurs and therefore overlook other equally important figures in the making of films – cinematographers, screenwriters, actors or composers, for example?

Bond films – *technically a sub-genre of* action films, *but virtually a genre of their own – are good examples of genre films. With these films, the tendency is to think of them more in terms of genre rather than, say, their director. How many directors of Bond films can you list?*

Films like* Taxi Driver (1976) *above,* Goodfellas (1990) *and* Casino (1995) *– all crime films, with* Goodfellas *and* Casino *being part of Scorsese's favoured gangster subgenre – tend to be thought of in terms of their director, Martin Scorsese.

7. Auteur approaches to film

Film Units

The principal cinematography on **American Beauty** *was by Conrad Hall. However his son headed a team who shot one short scene – Carolyn in her car at night towards the end of the film – which was used in the finished film.*

More on the authors of auteur...

Jim Hillier has edited a selection of articles from those early years of Cahiers du Cinéma. *Like* Sight and Sound, *the magazine is still published monthly.*

An extensive interview Truffaut made with Hitchcock was published in 1967 (see 'going further').

...and on the concept of auteur

Susan Haywood's entry on 'auteur' in Cinema Studies: Key Concepts *refers to earlier examples of the idea – in Germany in the 1910s and 20s, for example, where writers were seeking recognition of their role.*

A little more on how the idea of the 'auteur' first arose helps explain how those issues came about.

The authors of auteur and what they were reacting against

Hollywood films in particular, up until the early 1950s, were thought of as products of large film organisations, the 'studios', who produced films according to well-established practices. Most people who made films, particularly directors and cinematographers, were thought of as technicians, who delivered a product. Anybody, in the opinion of Hollywood producers, could direct a film, write a script or film it. Indeed, on films like producer David O Selznick's *Gone with the Wind* (1939), three directors were involved in the production (George Cukor, who later directed Marilyn Monroe in *Let's Make Love* (1960), Sam Wood of Marx Brothers' fame and Victor Fleming, who was at the time also working on *The Wizard of Oz* (1939)). There was rarely just one scriptwriter but teams of them (F. Scott Fitzgerald and Ben Hecht were among the many who worked on *Gone with the Wind*), to say nothing of cinematography, where there were frequently several 'film units' (as there are frequently today).

In the mid-1950s, a group of aspiring young French directors and film enthusiasts including Francois Truffaut, Alain Resnais and Jean-Luc Godard, set up their own film magazine which they called *Cahiers du Cinéma* (roughly translated – 'Cinema Notebooks'). They started looking at Hollywood films from the previous 20 years or so and claimed these films weren't simply industrial products manufactured by technicians but important 'works of art' by directors who fashioned their own style and tended to explore particular themes. They called these directors 'auteurs' ('authors') of their own works, giving them the status of literary writers, who had sole control over their own writing, generally with negligible interference from editors or the publishing firms they worked for.

They championed Alfred Hitchcock with his trademark suspense, created through taut narrative structures and editing, crosscutting and frequently highly inventive camera angles and fluent camera movement (some of the stylistic features running through his work); and his exploration of guilt and sexuality, often arguably voyeuristic (some of the thematic elements common to his films). Similarly they explored the work of Howard Hawks and his 'screwball' comedies (which had some influence on the more recent *Four Weddings and a Funeral* (1994)) and the Westerns of John Ford.

Truffaut, Resnais and Godard – to mention some of the main young directors – were drawing attention to the role of the director and tended therefore to imply that directors were more important than genres. That was the root of the tendency to value films shaped by directors more than 'genre' films.

Big brothers and sisters: directors as the supreme auteurs?

Cahiers emphasis on directors also tended to devalue the role of others who collaborated on the film and perhaps have a right to being considered crucial to the film. Think about the roles of all the people who exert a powerful influence over a film:

- the director – responsible for coordinating and guiding film-makers' contributions (responsible overall?);

- the cinematographer, responsible for the camerawork, lighting, composition of shots and thus the look of the film (or does she or he merely put into practice what the director wants?);

- the screenwriter, creator of story and dialogue and thus responsible for establishing the narrative and the major issues the film raises (or is it impossible to think of a script independently of the way it is turned into a film?);

- the set designer, responsible for the sets and establishing so much of the look of the film (or does she or he simply follow the director's ideas?);

- the producers, responsible for the finance of the film (or do they exert a strong influence over the film-makers and actors – not least because they frequently influence, even dictate, who is selected?);

- the actors (just following the script or responsible for interpreting it and thus creating characters who are important for the audience?);

- the composer (just providing background music or does the musical score give a distinctive atmosphere to the film and make action significant to audiences?).

When considering any of the above film-makers as an auteur, however, you are always asking some basic questions:

- what are the signature features of their work (stylistic and/or thematic)?

- how far are they responsible for their contribution?

- what does their contribution over several films suggest to audiences – what are the meanings created for them through their signature features?

American Beauty and auteurist approaches

Sam Mendes has to date only completed two films. Nevertheless, his work is already looking so distinctive that you might claim he is an auteur. Conrad Hall, the cinematographer (whose auteur credentials will be considered later), said that Sam Mendes had a clear 'vision' of *American Beauty* and thus hinted at Mendes' distinctive, auteur approach. Hall's comment almost literally points to an underlying feature of Mendes' work to date: it is marked by a strongly filmic and stylised visualisation of his subject-matter. Mendes, like Alan Ball and other directors like *American Beauty* screenwriter Vincente Minnelli in the 1940s, worked in the theatre prior to directing his first film. And what has characterised much of his stage work is that he has taken accessible, familiar and even popular works – like *Cabaret*, *Company*, *The Blue Room* or *Little Voice* – and produced stylised productions of them. There's a sense of trying to show the familiar in an unfamiliar way – or rely on audiences' familiarity with the subject-matter to shock them into seeing it in a new way.

Sam Mendes' signature features seem to me these:

- minimalist but highly suggestive mise-en-scène with an almost symbolic power;

- visual stylisation – reliance on studio-based camerawork, sparing but slow camera movement, slower pace of editing and increased length of shot and a tendency for symmetrical framing (this visual stylisation often creates the effect of seeing the familiar in an unfamiliar light);

- dramatic plotting and climaxes;

- an interest in links between potential voyeurism and film viewing;

- an assertion of the importance of family relationships amidst what seem to be unconventional 'family' structures.

I'll refer to some of the key signature scenes from *American Beauty* and *Road to Perdition* (1992) to explore these auteur features, suggest what meanings are created for audiences and raise some questions for research into how far either director or other figures are responsible for those features.

Signature moments of American Beauty and Road to Perdition

1: Minimalist but highly suggestive mise-en-scène with an almost symbolic power

An obvious comparison of minimalist mise-en-scène is the interview between

Brad and Lester in *American Beauty* (which I've referred to in section 2) and the interview between Frank Nitti (Stanley Tucci) and Michael (Tom Hanks) in *Road to Perdition*. Both are sparse and minimalist and both suggest a difference in power. This is arguably emphasised more in *American Beauty* by placing Lester in the centre of the room. In *Road to Perdition*, it is the inclusion of the desk, suggesting substantial power and the slightly lower angle from which Frank Nitti is shot, that achieves a similar effect.

The mise-en-scène in early sequences of both films suggests entrapment: in *American Beauty* Lester is constantly shot in enclosed spaces, within frames (e.g., behind the window frame, looking out) and even reflected in the vertical bar-like data on his computer screen at work. In *Road to Perdition*, the concentration on the young Michael's point of view moves gradually to his sense of entrapment after he witnesses the shooting. He is first framed trapped by the bars on the gates of

Working on auteurs – directors or other figures

1: Look for what is distinctive about the auteur you are exploring.

2: To start with, identify two stylistic and two thematic features.

3: Choose three films which support your ideas.

4: Choose at least one scene from each film which illustrates the features you have identified.

5: Question whether the distinctive features are solely the result of your chosen auteur's approach or whether they show influence from generic features or the filmic contributions of other significant figures involved in the making of the film.

6: Ask what is suggested to audiences by the auteur's approach – what meanings are created for them.

7. Auteur approaches to film

Mendes started out in the theatre like American Beauty writer Alan Ball.

His early productions were Chekhov's The Cherry Orchard at Chichester and Shakespeare's Troilus and Cressida, Richard III and The Tempest at the Royal Shakespeare Company.

...and like Vincente Minnelli in the 1940s

Minnelli, director of Meet Me in St Louis (1944), made the move from Broadway as a stage designer to Hollywood and brought with him an extravagant sense of set (to which he added highly fluent camerawork).

Classical, symmetrical framing

Conrad Hall, in his discussion of the storyboards on the American Beauty DVD, describes this symmetrical framing as 'bookend' framing, as though the left and right of the frame serve as bookends to the visual element in the centre.

Other examples of suggestive, minimalist mise-en-scène

American Beauty: dinner scene with the Burnhams – cold, empty set suggests emotional distance and emptiness (see section 2).

Road to Perdition: the breakfast scene suggests emotional closeness within a house which is threateningly empty.

the warehouse entrance (a medium close-up repeated three times), then within the frame of the car's back window before the 45 degree angle shot shows father and son confined in the car (with the frame of the car suggestively dividing father and son – a relatively long duration of shot). To punctuate the idea further, Michael is shown in bed looking at the bar-like reflection of the window on the ceiling. The cut to a tighter shot of the kitchen where the family ate breakfast, reprising, but contrasting with, the earlier shot of a warm, family gathering, suggests entrapment, which is emphasised by repeated shots of his mother through the frame of the window.

The later set-piece scene as father and son arrive in Chicago is another obvious example of overtly symbolic mise-en-scène. The oppressive power of Chicago and the smallness of both father and son is accentuated by the mise-en-scène. The shots are of Gothic-like skyscrapers – whose awesome power is emphasised by seeing them from the child Michael's point of view, first of all in reflection in the car's windows and then from low angles. Mendes clearly alludes to the classical filmic reference of that power of the city over insignificant individuals, Fritz Lang's 1926 Metropolis – a film contemporary with the setting of *Road to Perdition* of course. And the slow motion shots of thronging crowds in the streets, with father and son absorbed in the masses serves to emphasise that further. They are powerless and anonymous – the city is indifferent to their individual, painful circumstances, which is poignantly picked out as the young Michael is shown crying in the Reading Room as he reads the equally suggestive Lone Ranger. As Michael enters the hotel, the choice of rich interior, ornate and almost monumental at the same time, suggests power but also the corrupt illegality of the gangster world, confirmed to the audience by the minders guarding the lift.

Research into the extent of Mendes' auteur status

- Are there other directors who use mise-en-scène in similar ways?

- How significant is the example of German Expressionist film-makers and the film noir crime thrillers of the 1940s and 50s regarding use of mise-en-scène in suggestive ways?

- Is the director, the cinematographer or the set designer more important in establishing this use of mise-en-scène?

2: Visual stylisation (seeing the familiar in an unfamiliar way) – studio-based camerawork, sparing but slow camera movement, slower pace of editing and length of shot, symmetrical framing

The scenes mentioned above also demonstrate Mendes' stylised approach – the careful symmetrical composition of the meal scenes in both films, the central positioning of Lester being interviewed by Brad in *American Beauty* and the overt stylisation of the Chicago scene in *Road to Perdition*.

However, two further examples of Mendes' visual stylisation would be the use of slow motion. In *American Beauty* it is used for the fantasy sequences, populated with luscious rose petals, either pouring from Angela's breasts, floating down towards the prostrate Lester, providing a 'bed' for Angela or enveloping Angela in the bath. The visual stylisation of the slow motion sequences is also emphasised by sound – in this case, Thomas Newman's music.

In *Road to Perdition* a similar stylisation is used for the climactic killing of John Rooney (Paul Newman) and his associates – although it is the absence of sound which emphasises the stylisation here. Whereas in *American Beauty*, the slow motion is an obvious indication of fantasy, in *Road to Perdition* it hints at the unreal nature of violence as well as suggesting that the father–son relationship between Rooney and Michael is unreal in comparison with actual father–son and family relationships which motivates both to act in the way they do. (The slow movement of Rooney, as he turns to face Michael and his impending death has the feel of the moment where they play the piano duet earlier in the film – where action rather than camerawork is slowed.)

Research into the extent of Mendes' auteur status

- Are there other directors who are stylised in their approach in a similar way?

- Is it Mendes', the editor's or the cinematographer's role which is most distinctive in creating these moments of visual stylisation?

3: Dramatic plotting and climax

Both *American Beauty* and *Road to Perdition* are propelled by dramatic events which occur at similar moments within what are similar narrative structures. *American Beauty* moves towards an initial climactic turning point, which changes Lester's life: he sees and is completely mesmerised by Angela. The climax of the film is largely anticipated, if not caused by, the dramatically shocking moment in the garage as Fitts reveals his sexual orientation and feelings for Lester. The climax itself comes with the shooting of Lester.

With *Road to Perdition*, there are again three dramatic moments: the turning point shooting which Michael witnesses, the killing of Rooney by Michael which is the logical culmination of that train of events and the climactic killing of Michael by Maguire (Jude Law).

Mendes seems to be attracted to such shocking, dramatic plotting within the narratives and underlines them in film terms. They appear to be another signature feature of his work.

Research into the extent of Mendes' auteur status

- Are there other directors who incorporate similarly dramatic moments into their films and emphasise them strongly in filmic terms?

- Is this the result of Mendes' auteur signature or the screenwriter's?

4: Interest in voyeurism and film viewing

Mendes, like other directors before him, appears to be interested in raising questions about the parallels between film viewing and voyeurism. This is explored through Ricky and his digicam filming in *American Beauty* – looked at in the context of male gaze. In *Road to Perdition*, the role of sensationalist press photography and audiences' potential lurid fascination with the horrific is explored through Maguire's character. As discussed in section 6, Mendes seems to be playing with these ideas – raising questions in audiences' minds.

Research into the extent of Mendes' auteur status

- Is Mendes simply following other directors who have explored links between voyeurism and film spectators?

- How far is this a concern emphasised by Mendes or by the screenwriter?

5: An assertion of the importance of family relationships amidst what seem to be unconventional 'family' structures

Both *American Beauty* and *Road to Perdition* are based on the recognition of family ties. *American Beauty* climaxes with Lester's recognition of what is most important to him – his wife and child. Similarly, *Road to Perdition* is based on the lengths an individual will go to avenge his family's murder – but it is also crucially about the father and son bond, between Michael and his son and Rooney and his son in literal terms and more metaphorically between Rooney and Michael.

Expressionism

This use of mise-en-scène to express not only psychological states but also wider social and political concerns – like the insignificance of individuals within oppressive regimes – is rooted in German Expressionist film-making of the 1920s. Robert Wiene's The Cabinet of Dr Caligari *(1919) is a good example of a film conveying psychological states whilst Fritz Lang's* Metropolis *(1926) launches social and political criticism in visual terms.*

Expressionist lighting and visual stylisation in Lang's *Metropolis*: an influence on Mendes?

A contrasting use of sound, equally dramatic and disturbing, is the use of natural sound in Casino, *where Scorsese enhances the sound of the baseball bats striking bodies as the two brothers are clubbed to death.*

7. Auteur approaches to film

'Crime is my oyster' ('Weegee')

Maguire's role echoes that of 'Weegee's – Arthur Fellig – the photojournalist at work between the the 30s and the 60s but whose crime photographs of the 30s and 40s are most famous. He worked closely with the police, being first at the scene and concerned to get the right shot – although not with the ruthlessness of Maguire.

Mendes in the future

In February 2004, Mendes set up a new film, TV and theatre company, 'Scamp', which has a 'first look' arrangement with DreamWorks over potential projects but already has rights to film Khaled Hosseini's The Kite Runner, an Afghanistan-set novel.

Conrad Hall as auteur?

Conrad Hall is something of a veteran cinematographer. He started working with a camera in the late 40s. Influenced by John Alton he photographed a number of significant films in the 1960s, including Cool Hand Luke (1967), In Cold Blood (1967) and the Oscar award-winning Butch Cassidy and the Sun Dance Kid (1969).

Other films include Marathon Man (1976) – which Mendes makes a visual reference to in American Beauty – Black Widow (1987), Tequila Sunrise (1988) and Mendes' second film, Road to Perdition.

Two scenes where that emerges are Lester attempting to engage with Jane in the kitchen, following the first dinner scene in American Beauty; and Michael speaking to his son at the farm, for the first time trying to find out about his son. Both demonstrate the importance of the bond between parents and children.

Research into the extent of Mendes' auteur status

- What other directors seem to place such emphasis on family?

- How distinctive is Mendes' handling of this issue

- How far is this a concern emphasised by Mendes or by the screenwriter?

Cinematographer Conrad Hall as auteur

One of the most significant contributors to both of Sam Mendes' films is the cinematographer, Conrad Hall. His approach to cinematography I think makes him an auteur. However, cinematographers represent a particularly interesting area to research as they embody the central debate underlying auteur approaches: are they being individual and distinctive or just putting into practice directors' visions?

Sven Nykvist, a cinematographer who worked most notably with Ingmar Bergman, claims he's a collaborator:

> 'The most important task of the cinematographer is to create an atmosphere….the cinematographer… has the task of carrying out the intentions of the script and catching the moods and feeling that the director wants to convey…Every situation is different and collaboration is a major part of film-making.'
>
> Nykvist in Bergery, 2002

Vittorio Storaro, who has worked most with Bernardo Bertolucci, claimed on the other hand that he was an auteur:

> '…cinematography means writing with light in movement. Cinematographers are authors of photography, not

directors of photography. We are not merely using technology to convey someone else's thoughts because we are also using our own emotions, cultures, and inner beings.'
>
> Storaro in Bergery, 2002

Everything Conrad Hall has said publicly seems to suggest that he sees himself as following Mendes' auteurist vision. One might claim, however, that it was precisely Conrad Hall's distinctive lighting and composition that enabled him to put into practice what Sam Mendes wanted. Hall's approach is based on the expressionist lighting of *film noir*, which John Alton documented in his ground-breaking *Painting with Light* (written in 1949, at the height of his film noir cinematography).

Hall's signature lighting and composition

Hall's signature lighting and composition comes down to this:

- favours lighting figures from behind (backlighting, reflected lighting) to create natural shadows, silhouetted faces and less dense lighting in foreground;

- unpretentious camerawork, which incorporates slight variations in angles and camera movement within sequences of shots;

- aims always to exploit depth of vision;

- classical composition, whether that is symmetrical or clearly balanced.

Hall himself sums up his distinctive approach to lighting like this:

> 'Lighting is all just painting and creating depth. It's being cognizant of the light's values in black-and-white. In black-and-white photography, you have to create depth to create a sense of reality. In color, I still want to create depth, but I don't like to do that with the colors. I don't like the separation in an image to be due to the fact that a couch is gray and the walls are orange. Instead, I do it by treating the colors as values of gray and then lighting for depth.'
>
> (*American Cinematographer*, March 2000)

This creates an effect of softer lighting, with

no harsh lines between figures and objects, and expressive shadows. An unpretentious example of all those signature features comes in *American Beauty* when Carolyn comes to speak with Jane in Jane's bedroom. Indeed, when he mentions the orange walls, he may well be thinking of this scene. You see:

- depth of shot as you are aware of the complete room with its orange walls but not demarcated from the other colours of the room;

- backlighting, which attempts to replicate the low-level lighting in Jane's bedroom, and which creates silhouetted faces of mother and daughter;

- slightly angled reverse shots (to underline the angular tension between mother and daughter at this point);

- a pan to follow Carolyn as she moves towards Jane, emphasising her attempt to reach out to her daughter;

- classical composition in the simple juxtaposition of mother and daughter in preparation of Carolyn's slapping of her daughter, following her daughter's rejection of her mother's attempt at a 'Kodak moment'.

All of these signature features run throughout Conrad Hall's work. It is a style of camerawork, which as said, traces a heritage from German Expressionist film-makers, like Wiene, Murnau and Lang, through film noir directors, like Billy Wilder (*Double Indemnity* (1944), *Sunset Boulevard* (1950)), Edgar Ulmer (*Detour* (1945)) Robert Siodmak (*The Spiral Staircase* (1946), *The Killers* (1946), *Cry of the City* (1948)), John Alton (*T-Men* (1947) and *The Big Combo* (1955, Joseph H. Lewis, director)) and Robert Aldrich (*Kiss Me Deadly* (1955)) to Orson Welles' work. *Touch of Evil* (1958) is Welles' film noir, but he used expressionist camerawork in all his films, very transparently, however, in *Citizen Kane* (1941), where Gregg Toland was the cinematographer, a notable influence on Conrad Hall. All of these figures had a significant impact on Hall – notably those shot by John Alton or Gregg Toland. You see it not only in his films of the 1960s where you might expect to – the crime-based *Cool Hand Luke* and *In Cold Blood* – but also in Westerns such as *Butch Cassidy and the Sundance Kid*, which (like *Road to Perdition* and *Cool Hand Luke*) featured Paul Newman.

The two sequences which introduce first Butch Cassidy (Paul Newman) and then the Sundance Kid (Robert Redford) are seeped in his trademark cinematography. Both were shot in black and white, to which a sepia tint was added, there is an emphasis on close-ups, backlighting and sidelighting, particularly when Butch walks towards, and is framed within, the doorframe of the bank – presumably a conscious echo of the closing shot of *The Searchers* (1956). The backlight just illuminates Butch to create silhouettes, you're aware of the depth of focus through the doorway. The camerawork concentrates on medium shots and close-ups and the composition is balanced with Butch central, the security guard to the right and space to left.

The symmetrical composition and lighting are even more apparent when the Sundance Kid is introduced. The shot focuses on the Sundance Kid in close-up, framed with the shadows of the other two figures playing cards left and right. The Sundance Kid is backlit with sidelighting, producing a natural shadow. Indeed, the shot is held for over a minute and a quarter – an extraordinary length of time. As Robert L Crawford, associate producer, and George Roy Hill, director, both commented, Hall used to have a preference for backlighting and Rembrandt-like chiaroscuro effects, which he used to prepare for very carefully. (All of the shots in *Butch Cassidy* which required Hall's elaborate set ups were produced on studio backlots.)

Road to Perdition adopts a similar stylistic approach. In addition to just about all those mentioned so far, the scene where Michael wakes up his son to signal their departure from the farm and the moment when we are first introduced to Maguire as he photographs the murderer, are both filmed with all Hall's signature approaches to lighting.

Conrad Hall himself analyses the final scene between Lester and Angela in *American Beauty* and shows how he creates these signature features in an interview with Christopher Probst for the cinematographer's magazine, *American Cinematographer* (2000), extracted below:

Conrad Hall supporting Mendes as an auteur – professional respect or significant evidence?

'Everything fell into place because Sam Mendes had such a clear vision of where to take this story; that made all of us contribute not three different visions – referring to director, cinematographer and designer – but to one vision. All of our work fit into what he was trying to achieve with Alan Ball's incredible script.'

'...what makes absolutely wonderful cinema is when the collaborative process comes together in a way that is artfully appropriate for that particular story. I felt that way about American Beauty.*'*

- Christopher Probst, 'Impeccable Images', American Cinematographer, June 2000

Conrad Hall seems to think that Sam Mendes, even in his first film, approached the film in an auteur-like way. As Mendes' film-making progresses, it will doubtless become clearer.

7. Auteur approaches to film

The three main sources of light generally used are variations on the following:

Key light – main source of light, generally in front of the scene.

Fill light – to fill in shadows, give tone, generally to the side of a scene.

Back light – lighting behind a scene, which can pick out shapes of objects and bodies and create silhouettes.

Conrad Hall's lighting

'He lights as dark as he can and then prints the image "up" to compensate...' (Sam Mendes)

'That gives you more texture. But it also makes the actors a lot more comfortable. The lower the light, the cooler the set. I heard Stanley Kubrick did that on Eyes Wide Shut.' (Hall explaining Mendes' comment, both quoted in American Cinematographer, Mar 2000)

film noir – *French for 'dark film', where 'dark' refers to the shadowy world created by its low-key lighting*

Films noir were largely private eye-based crime thrillers, where low-key lighting created the shadowy world of the criminal underbelly of American society. An emphasis on single sources of lights – back-lighting and side-lighting – created the shadows and silhouettes, as did such props as Venetian blinds which naturally filtered shafts of light from the outside world.

Shot 1: Lester entering room, standing in doorway in silhouette, with light on his face

On the right side of frame, I had a special light just edging the bouquet of roses. Throughout the entire picture, I made a conscious effort to feature the roses in frame. In fact, the set dressers had roses everywhere – they're in almost every shot – but keeping them bright red and all lit up could become pretty boring and too obvious a gimmick. Instead, I usually tried to keep them dark [or just light] the back edge of them to keep them black, while just giving them a little red tinge.

Shot 2: Wide shot of Angela on left and Lester on right, facing one another, silhouetted against the French windows with the rain outside

Ultimately, I worked with the same sort of strategy I always do – I first light for what I want to see by painting in specific areas in values of black and white, and then add a final light that I call 'room-tone.' Room-tone is a fill light, usually bounced from the ceiling off a beadboard or white card, that brings up the shadows to where I want them – without really showing the presence of the fill, while still keeping the blacks black.

Shot 1

Shot 2

Shot 3

We had some special material on the windows to make the water run a bit slower, which also helps pick up highlights. In this shot, the windows actually get way too bright for a night scene, but I let them

go. It's almost scary to have something so bright in there, but to me, beauty comes from contrast. I love contrast – either the lack of it, or an abundance of it. I always love having hot elements in the frame when it's appropriate. In truth, reality isn't always perfectly balanced. I love to have images that are a bit over-the-top – either too light or too dark – because they provide energy and a more 'realistic' dynamic range.

It's almost a black-and-white picture with a dash of red in it.

Shot 3: Wider two-shot of Lester and Angela, with light on Angela's back

In this wider two-shot, the light on the wall in the background, the light on her back and the light to the left on the couch gives the image a very structured kind of composition. It's very simple. It gives you peace and comfort to have a frame that's looser and allows you to breathe.

The light on Mena's shoulder at frame right is supposed to be coming from the porch-light coming in through the window, but it was most likely generated by a 1Kilowatt Baby with a lot of wire on it, or a Tweenie shining through a rain-box inside the room. I used rainboxes all over the place. That way, you can place a rain pattern anywhere you want without lighting the whole damn room.

Research into how far Conrad Hall is an auteur

- Are there other cinematographers who approach lighting in this way?
- Is Hall responsible for this approach or is he responding to directors' visions?

Auteur features to consider

- Ball's screenplays are informed by the situation comedy genre – a concentration on domestic situation, a limited range of characters and a humorous tone.
- His screenplays are characterised by grotesque humour and a sense of the surreal within the real.
- There is frequently a sense of restless sexuality underlying characters.
- Characters are shown having to confront significant events in their lives, leading to changes in their own outlooks.
- His writing integrates gay characters unpretentiously, gay sexuality seen as part of everyday life.

Questions to raise

- Are there other writers producing similar material?
- Is Alan Ball responsible for these auteur features or are they a response to what producers and directors want?
- How far does a script rely on a director or cinematographer to visualise it in film terms?

Rembrandt-like chiaroscuro effects...

'Chiaroscuro' is the Italian for mixing dark with light and refers to artists like Rembrandt who pictures light coming from one source – e.g., The Night Watchman's Lamp (1642) – and which thus creates natural shadows.

John Alton drew attention to the influence of Rembrandt and other painters of the 17th century on his own 'chiaroscuro' lighting in his book, Painting with Light.

These film noir effects have been enormously influential since. Some obvious examples are Roman Polanski's Chinatown (1974), Kathryn Bigelow's Blue Steel (1990), David Fincher's Se7en and David Lynch's Lost Highway, which builds in references to Robert Aldrich's Kiss Me Deadly.

Other possible auteurs to explore

Alan Ball, screenwriter

It may seem a paradox to explore the work of a screenwriter to consider whether he or she is an 'auteur' but screenwriters in film terms are frequently the most overlooked, even though the script is the starting point for a film. In Alan Ball's case, however, his name has been quite widely publicised and he has subsequently created, produced and occasionally directed the television series, *Six Feet Under* (2001 onwards), originally marketed as being from the 'writer of *American Beauty*'. It's equally significant that in *American Beauty*, for instance, he was a co-producer and for the sitcom *Cybill* he had also been a producer.

Thomas Newman, composer

Another less obvious, but challenging approach to an auteur, would be to explore the composer, Thomas Newman. His credits include *Desperately Seeking Susan* (1985), *Jumpin' Jack Flash* (1986), *Josh and S.A.M.* (1993), *Unstrung Heroes* (1995), *Less Than Zero* (1997), *Finding Nemo* (2003) and the main titles music for *Six Feet Under*.

7. Auteur approaches to film

'American Beauty *is a hilarious, sad and somewhat disturbing picture that ultimately affirms a sense of our humanity. However, the whole film has a certain sense of peace compositionally, and a sort of classicism. Everything is quiet and simple, which allows the viewer to just watch things happen in a very graphic frame.'*
Christopher Probst,
American Cinema,
March 2000

Auteur features to consider

- Minimalist scores, which aim to capture dry humour as well as emotional intensity:

'Every cue is constructed out of small, endlessly repeating phrases, with little variation (a simple thinning of the texture often suffices) and few modulations.'

(James Tomiainen,
Film Score Monthly, February 2000)

- A commitment to pulse, rhythm and colour over melody.

- The use of percussive textures, tuned and detuned – like the marimbas, metal mixing bowls and detuned mandolin.

- A linking of music to particular ideas (a kind of 'Leitmotif', to use the classical term introduced by 19th century opera composer, Richard Wagner).

'It is these colours (the single breath of a flute, or a shimmering, glass-like electronic whisper) that define Newman's style and take this score to deeper emotional levels. The simple open fifths of the piano…delicately accompanied by string orchestra, make for a sense of tragic integrity.'

(James Tomiainen, ibid)

Questions to raise

- What kind of contribution does Thomas Newman's music make to *American Beauty*?

- What is distinctive about Newman's approach? Or do other composers produce music of a similar style?

'And Janie... And Janie... And Carolyn.'

Looking closer: what Lester finally realises are the most important things in his 'stupid little life'.

NOTES:

Going further – bibliography and filmography

This guide is as much about studying *American Beauty* as it is about studying film in general. I've concentrated on the following areas:

- micro and macro features of film
- the film industry and how that shapes films (the production, distribution and exhibition of films)
- audiences – different kinds of audience – and the potentially different ways different audiences respond to and make sense of films
- film-makers and their status (auteurs)

Below are several suggestions about going further with these approaches, which I've grouped together under those areas. I've tried to mention some more general material on film as well as refer to the material I found most helpful in approaching *American Beauty*.

A few guides

The Virgin Film Guide – generally very informative entries on individual films and updated annually.

Rough Guide to Cult Movies (*Rough Guides, 2001*)

There are brief entries on *American Beauty* in both of the above.

More from the web

For all internet research, one of the best search engines is:

- Google – www.google.com

And amongst the more obvious film-based sites, www.imdb.com and www.channel4.com/film are two good places to start. But I would always recommend searching with Google.

More articles and books

However, don't forget that there are numerous articles and books not available on the web. I've listed some of the main articles and books which I've referred to. There are one or two slightly more challenging items but the majority are not difficult to understand.

More on the film's micro and macro features (relates to sections 2 and 3 of this guide)

Rick Altman, *Film/Genre* (BFI Publishing, 1999)

Benjamin Bergery, *Reflections: 21 Cinematographers at Work* (ASC Press, Hollywood, 2002)

Gill Branston & Roy Stafford, *The Media Student's Book* (Routledge, 2003)

Kate Domaille, *The Horror Genre* (Auteur Publishing, 2001)

Rob Feld, 'Answered Prayers: The Indie Film's Identity Crisis', *Written By*, Dec/Jan 2000

Susan Hayward, *Cinema Studies: Key Concepts* (Routledge, 2000)

Philip Kemp, 'The Iceman Cometh', *Sight and Sound*, January 2000

Geoff King, *New Hollywood* (IB Tauris, 2002)

Nick Lacey, *Narrative and Genre* (Macmillan, 2000)

Nick Lacey, *Image and Representation* (Macmillan, 1998)

Leitch and Greenhalgh (eds), *Making Pictures: A Century of European Cinematography* (Aurum Press, 2002)

Richard Maltby, *Hollywood Cinema* (1995; 2nd edition, 2003)

Sam Mendes & Alan Ball, Audio commentary on film (*American Beauty* DVD, 2000, extra)

Sam Mendes, Storyboard Discussions (*American Beauty* DVD, 2000, extra)

Patrick Phillips, *Understanding Film Texts: Meaning and Experience* (BFI Publishing, 2000)

Cherry Potter, 'Multiple Protagonists with Conflicting or Separate Aims: Mendes' *American Beauty*' in her *Screen Language: From Film Writing to Film-making* (Methuen, 2001)

Jeffrey Sconce, 'Irony, Nihilism and the New American Smart Film', *Screen* 43:4, Winter 2002

Kristin Thompson, *Storytelling in Film and TV* (Harvard University Press, 2003)

More on the film industry – production, distribution & exhibition (section 5 of this guide)

Two theatrical release trailers (*American Beauty* DVD, 2000, extra)

www.americanbeauty.com (at time of going to press, still available on the web)

British Video Assocation Yearbook (published annually)

Thomas Austin, *Hollywood, Hype and Audiences* (Manchester University Press, 2002)

Peter N Chumo II, 'An Interview with Alan Ball', *Creative Screenwriting*

Eddie Dyja (ed.), *BFI Film and Television Handbook 2004* (BFI Publishing, 2003) – annual publication, collects range of statistics from two years prior to publication in the introduction

Entertainment Weekly, 'Wes Bentley', 8 Oct 1999

Nicholas Kazan, 'True Beauty', *Written By*, March 2000

Leonard Klady, 'The *Beauty* of Platform Success', *Variety*, 4-10 Oct 99

John Pierson, *Spike, Mike, Slackers and Dykes: A Guided Tour across a Decade of Independent American Cinema* (Faber, 1995)

Mark Readman, *Teaching Scriptwriting, Screenplays and Storyboards for Film and TV Production* (BFI Education, 2003) – includes some useful approaches to screenwriting, with references to some of the screenwriting 'classics'

Going further – bibliography and filmography

More on audiences (section 6 of this guide)

Vivienne Clarke, *Studying* The Piano (Auteur, 2005)

John Fiske, 'The Cultural Economy of Fandom' in Lisa Lewis (ed), *The Adoring Audience: Fan Culture and Popular Media* (Routledge, 1992)

Sarah Gilligan, *Teaching Women and Film* (BFI Education, 2004)

Henry Jenkins, '"Strangers no more, we sing": Filking and the Social construction of the Science Fiction Fan Community' in Lisa Lewis (ed), *The Adoring Audience* (Routledge, 1992)

Jill Nelmes, 'Women and Film', *Introduction to Film Studies* (3rd edition, Routledge, 2003)

Melvyn Stokes & Richard Maltby, *Identifying Hollywood's Audiences* (BFI Publishing, 1999)

Melvin Stokes & Richard Maltby, *Hollywood Spectatorship: Changing Perceptions of Cinema Audiences* (BFI Publishing, 2001)

Fan sites can most easily be accessed via www.google.com

More about the film-makers and their status as auteurs (Mendes, Hall and Newman in particular)

John Alton, *Painting with Light* (University of California Press, 1995, first published 1949)

Lawrence Friedman, *The Cinema of Martin Scorsese* (Roundhouse, Oxford, 1997)

Susan Hayward, *Cinema Studies: Key Concepts* (Routledge, 2000), entry on 'Auteur' (discusses earlier usages of 'auteur' idea prior to Cahiers group)

Jim Hillier (ed.), *Articles from Cahiers du Cinema* (BFI Publishing, 2000)

Jim Hillier & Peter Wollen (eds), *Howard Hawks: American Artist* (BFI Publishing, 1997)

Andre Laudé, *Weegee* (Thames and Hudson, 1989)

Sam Mendes, 'One of the Few Genuine Artists I Have Known', tribute to Hall after his death, *Guardian*, 17 January 2003

Christopher Probst, 'Impeccable Images', *American Cinematographer*, June 2000

Stuart Samuels, Andrew and Arnold Glassman, *Visions of Light: The Art of Cinematography* (video/DVD, 1992)

Thomas Schatz, *Hollywood Genres: Formulas, Filmmaking and The Studio System* (McGraw Hill, 1981)

James Tomiainen, Review of soundtrack to *American Beauty, Film Score Monthly*, February 2000

Francois Truffaut, *Hitchcock/Truffaut* (Truffaut's 1967 interview with Hitchcock) in ed Helen Scott, *Hitchcock* (Simon and Schuster, 1985)

David Thompson and Ian Christie, *Scorsese on Scorsese* (Faber, revised 2004)

other films / TV

Sam Mendes, *Road to Perdition* (2002)

Six Feet Under (2001 onwards) – TV series created and produced by Alan Ball based around the work and lives of a West Coast family-owned funeral parlour

Influences on Sam Mendes

Billy Wilder, *Sunset Boulevard* (1951)

Billy Wilder, *The Apartment* (1960)

Robert Redford, *Ordinary People* (1980)